M. S. Ew&ing

CW00660494

introducing
catholic
theology

introducing catholic theology

Clare
Richards

kevin
mayhew

First published in 2002 by
KEVIN MAYHEW LTD
Buxhall, Stowmarket, Suffolk IP14 3BW
Email: info@kevinmayhewltd.com

9 8 7 6 5 4 3 2 1 0

ISBN 1 84003 962 0
Catalogue No 1500536

Cover design by Angela Selfe
Edited by Lesley Butland
Typesetting by Louise Selfe
Printed and bound in Great Britain

Contents

Preface 7

1 The Bible: Old Testament 9

2 The Bible: New Testament 23

3 Jesus Christ 33

4 The Church 49

5 The Sacraments 69

6 Christian Morality 87

Notes for those writing essays 105

Acknowledgements 107

Preface

As the title of the book suggests, this is no more than an introduction to Roman Catholic theology. The problem I had in preparing it was to keep the ideas and language as simple as possible. This is not easy to do without, in some way, oversimplifying complex ideas, which could lead to inaccuracies. I persevered because I am convinced that most theological books are quite off-putting to the non-specialist.

A book that is just a 'taster' seems necessary. Over many years I have come to realise that most Catholics have had no access to the development of theology, especially to the progress made in recent years in biblical theology. My own faith has been deepened by the insights and vision of the Church brought about by the Second Vatican Council. It is now a generation on since the Council, yet many Catholics remain almost unaware of developed theology.

This small book only claims to *introduce* the reader to Catholic theology. I have in mind interested adults and students who are studying for the Catholic Certificate in Religious Studies (CCRS), awarded by the Bishops' Conference of England and Wales. The book is designed to give a brief, overall view of the course. The six sections are based on the six core modules. Of course, students for the award will need to move on to more detailed texts and appropriate titles are recommended.

There are others who may be grateful for a simple explanation of contemporary theology – teachers, deacons in training, adult education groups, parish discussion groups and individuals who seek to deepen their personal faith.

I was invited this year by a Norfolk parish to give a short course in theology as a preparation for Easter. I used the manuscript for this book as my source material. It was a great pleasure to share post-Vatican II ideas with the large group of (mostly) senior citizens on our Tuesday afternoons. It is a sad reflection on the pattern of our Catholic lives that several participants asked why they had 'never really heard this before'. They were excited by new thinking and by having the chance to question old ideas. The experience deepened our faith and our sense of community.

I would like to dedicate the book to Fr Peter Marsh and my new friends in the 'Church at North Walsham'.

1

The Bible: Old Testament

*The Lord blessed Sarah, as he had promised, and she became
pregnant and bore a son to Abraham when he was old.*
Genesis 21:1-2

Introduction to the Bible

What does the Bible mean to you? Word of God and word of humans – which aspect is predominant? With which do you start? What is the right balance? The sacred and / or the secular? Inerrancy?

Orientation

Many of our difficulties with the Bible stem from the *western* mentality that we bring to it: argument, logic, explanation, abstract, literal. The Bible (both testaments) is totally *eastern*: action, concrete, dramatic.

It is *about* people from the East, and *written by* people from the East. It tells of people *doing*: Adam and Eve, Cain and Abel, Noah, Abraham, Moses, kings, prophets.

This continues into the New Testament: at Cana, in Samaria, in the desert, at the pool, on the lake, etc. Even Jesus' 'explanations' are further stories of Samaritans, Pharisees, prodigals, shepherds and bridesmaids. These stories are told *not* to inform, but to convey a meaning, make a point. If we don't get on to *that* wavelength, reading the Bible is a waste of time. We would completely miss the point.

This Biblical 'orientation' is already suggested in the names originally given to the books:

- Genesis, Exodus, Leviticus, Numbers and Deuteronomy were called *Torah* – instruction in a way of life.

- Joshua, Judges, Samuel and Kings were called *Prophets* – preaching through illustrations.

- Matthew, Mark, Luke and John were called *Gospels* – good news to shout about.

Literary forms

A random selection of short texts from the Old and New Testaments will illustrate the vast variety of 'literary forms' they contain; these are lost if all are read in the same tone of voice. For example, 1-2 Samuel is *history*, Leviticus is all *legislation*, Acts 15:36-28:22 is a *diary*, Matthew 13:4-9 is a *story*, Nehemiah 1:5-11 is a *prayer*,

Isaiah 6 is a *vision*, Numbers 33 is an *itinerary*, Genesis 5 is a *genealogy*, Exodus 15 is a *song*, 1 Chronicles 16 is a *hymn*, Song of Songs 2:8-14 is a *love poem*, Philemon is a *personal letter*, Acts 2:14-36 is a *sermon*, Psalm 73 (72) is a *theological reflection*, Ecclesiastes 1-2 is an *essay*. Not one book, but a shelfful. If these are not first seen as pieces of human literature, how can we hear what God may be saying through them?

Presence of Christ

And yet we have bound this rich variety together in a single book, often in a richly decorated binding, to have it venerated with awe in the liturgy (especially Orthodox), almost as if it were a person. And this is precisely what Christians believe: both Bible and Christ are given the same title – 'Word of God'.

Obviously this must not be understood crudely. Even Christ comes among us in a thoroughly human form, and dies as all humans do.

Even so, Christians treasure the Bible as a presence of Christ, and read its stories of creation, exodus, temple, exile, preaching and healing as events in the present, not the past.

Truth

How *true* is the Bible? W. Keller's *Bible as History* contains much archaeological evidence of the Bible's accuracy about past events. But he is silent on its many historical inaccuracies! The fact is, the Bible does not claim to be an authority on history, geography or biology. It is not concerned with how, when or where: it always asks the deeper questions: who and why? It does not claim to be true to facts, but true to life, true to experience, true to God.

In many instances, the same story is even told in two or three different forms: the Feeding of the Thousands; Abraham and Sarah repeat the story of Isaac and Rebekah; mankind's place in creation in Genesis 1 and 2; monarchy good or bad in 1 Samuel, for example. *Remember*: the Bible is not concerned with how, when, or where – only with who and why.

New Testament versus Old Testament

Is the Old Testament all wrath, justice, anger, war? Is the New Testament all joy, mercy, love, peace?

Just compare Mark 9:45f, Matthew 25:41f, Revelation 14:8f (all wrath) with Psalm 103 (102):8f, Jeremiah 31:20f, Song of Songs 7:6f (all joy). What Jesus preached was the God he found in the Old Testament. Some pages of the Old Testament (and of the New!) distort that picture.

Divine or human?

Both the Bible and Jesus are given the title 'Word of God'. Jesus was neither man full stop, nor God full stop, nor half of each, but totally both: the whole truth about God lived out in the life of an ordinary man. The same must be said about the Bible: fully divine without ceasing to be fully human, the whole truth about God expressed in ordinary (and therefore fallible) human terms.

Here is a record of how our family have understood what God asks of them and calls them to. In the light of that, we must ask what he calls *us* to.

The Law – a guide for living

The first five books of the Bible (Greek *pentateuchos*) are known by Jews as the *Torah*, or Law, or guide for living. Scholars agree that they are an intricate weaving together of four strands or traditions. It helps to disentangle them, and examine each individually.

Yahwistic tradition (J)

This earliest tradition has little law (Exodus 34) and is composed mostly of stories. These, however, all have a doctrinal content, their main purpose being to express the relationship between Yahweh and mankind.

The description of Yahweh, almost always in human terms (see

Genesis 2-3: potter, gardener, judge, tailor), expresses his closeness to us in terms of friendship (grace). Yet he remains a transcendent God (Exodus 3:2-5, 4:10-11) and for humans to try to be his equal is disaster (Genesis 2-3). Nevertheless, this sovereignty does not swamp his love and mercy (Genesis 18:22-32), and sin is immediately followed by Yahweh's pardon (Genesis 3:14-15, 4:13-15, 6:7-8).

In short the Yahwist is a theologian, teaching us our relationship to God and answering our problems (Genesis 2-3). This theology is told in the Bible's most colourful stories (see Genesis 18, 24 and 27).

The traditions are clearly rooted in the events themselves. The written document dates from about 1000 BC, before schism and trouble, with a strong emphasis on Judah.

Yahweh God fashioned man out of clay, and breathed into him the breath of life.

Elohistic tradition (E)

From Genesis 12, E runs parallel with J. Its name for God (*Elohim*, plural of majesty and extension) expresses a more developed theology. God is less familiar, revealing himself in terrible majesty so that the very place becomes holy (Exodus 3:1, 4, 6 and 19:16-19); or remotely in dreams (Jacob and Joseph). Such an invisible God must not be represented (Genesis 35:1-4; Exodus 20:4, 23). His name *Yahweh*, revealed later, means the 'inexpressible mystery' (Exodus 3:13, 32:15-28).

E's morality is similarly more developed (compare J and E in Abraham's saving of Sarah, in Jacob's revenge on Laban, and in the plan to rescue Joseph).

E has preserved more law, namely Exodus 21-23, the code of the Sinai Covenant. Primitive and simple, it expresses duty to God (worship only in places made holy by his presence) and to each other (parallel to other contemporary legislation, but infinitely more moderate, as seen in Exodus 21-22).

The emphasis on Joseph (Genesis 37-) suggests that it comes from the Northern Kingdom about 800 BC, reflecting the efforts of Elijah and Elisha to present the full religious force of the old traditions.

Joseph had another dream, and he said: 'The sun and the moon and the stars bowed down before me.'

Deuteronomic tradition (D)

Though this deals entirely with legislation, it throbs with life. Ancient history is read over, and its meaning searched to reveal Yahweh throughout as the God of the Covenant who has chosen Israel freely (Deuteronomy 4:32-34, 7:7) and protected and blessed her (7:13-20). Israel's keeping of his law cannot be a burden but only a return of love for love (6:4-9), something very close to her heart (30:11-14). This love of God necessarily overflows into love of neighbour (10:18-19, 15:7-11, 24-25).

Yahweh's love is that of a husband, jealous of rivals, and demanding total commitment. The various sanctuaries, therefore, which had confused his worship with that of Canaanite Baals, must give way to the one and only sanctuary at Jerusalem (12:5-7). Since such legislation was not in force until 620 BC (Josiah), (though utterly dependent on the work and spirit of Moses), the book can be dated about 700 BC, the result of the long spiritual formation of Amos, Hosea, Isaiah and Jeremiah. The books of Joshua, Judges, Samuel and Kings are from the same school.

Yahweh, your God, loves you.

Priestly tradition (P)

Drier, more systematic, cold and repetitious (cf. Genesis 5:6f, Exodus 26:1f), this tradition emphasises the liturgy, priesthood and laws of worship. Like J, it goes back to Adam, to show history in the light of successive covenants (Adam, Noah, Abraham) linked up in an orderly and selective manner (*'These are the generations'*, Genesis 2:4, 5, 10, etc.) and systematically numbered.

It comes to a climax in the great lawgiver, Moses, whose legislation for desert worship is the nucleus of later legislation on priesthood and Temple (here grouped around his name: Exodus 25-40; Leviticus; Numbers 1-10). All stories are told to point to some legislation (creation – Sabbath; Abraham – circumcision; plagues – Paschal liturgy).

This meticulous emphasis on Law makes P colder than J, E and D. Its power comes from its overwhelming stress on God's transcendence, unapproachableness, holiness or otherness. That such a God has pitched his tent among Israel demands from them a similar holiness and otherness (Exodus 29:45; Leviticus 19:2, 20:22, 26). Israel is a Church, whose whole life is a liturgy. Such a deeply spiritual concept was only evolved in exile, under the influence of the priest-prophet Ezekiel, about 540 BC. It had its effect on Chronicles, Ezra, Nehemiah. And down to the Judaism of New Testament times.

Be holy, because I am holy.

The Editor (Redactor)

The Exile took away from Israel all else but its traditions. It was here that they were finally put together, in eastern manner, by interleaving without changing. The result is, therefore, not a mere record of the past, but a collection of what is finest in Israel's traditions. As such it was called the *Torah* or Law, the expression of God's will which would act as a yardstick for their lives. Ezra's first public presentation of this total picture caused tears of remorse and joy (Nehemiah 8:1-12). As the Word of God, dwelling amongst us, it was the focal point of Judaism (Psalms 19 and 119), perfected (not abolished) by Christ's coming (Matthew 5:17-19).

The Law of Yahweh is my delight, I meditate on it all the day.

The Prophets

The second section of the Old Testament is called *The Prophets*, and begins (unexpectedly) *not* with Isaiah, Jeremiah, etc., but with Joshua, Judges, Samuel and Kings, as much as to say, 'These stories too are told, not because x, y and z happened, but because they teach us how we are related to God – through love' (the theme of the Deuteronomist).

- **Joshua** is the sequel to the Exodus story: 'the Saviour' leads his people into the Promised Land, 1250 BC.

- **Judges** reflects on the period 1200 to 1050 BC, less optimistically, though God forgives seventy times seven.
- **Samuel – Kings** cover 1050 to 550 BC, and tell of the difficulties of establishing God's Kingdom on earth: the ambiguity of Samuel, failure of Saul, success of David (Son of God), Solomon's Temple, decline of both southern and northern kingdoms, the first prophets, and finally exile – the inevitable result (according to the Deuteronomistic author) of unfaithfulness.

The 'Major' prophets appear in the Bible in order of length:

- **Isaiah 1-39** (700 BC) commends blind trust in God (*Yesha – Yahu* means 'salvation comes from Yahweh'), and introduces the young king Hezekiah as a pledge that 'God is on our side' (*Immanu El*).
- **Isaiah 40-55** (Deutero-Isaiah: 550 BC) offers consolation to the exiles in Babylonia and promises a return under a renewed Israel – the Suffering Servant willing to die in order to bring the world to God.
- **Isaiah 56-66** (400 BC) criticises the narrow outlook of his contemporaries (see also Jonah below).
- **Jeremiah** (600 BC) presides over the destruction of Jerusalem. He is the 'man of sorrows' who saves his people through his suffering. Yet he too offers consolation (see chapters 30-31).
- **Ezekiel** (600 BC), the frail 'son of man', rallies the exiles with hope of a new Jerusalem presided over by a new priesthood.

The 'Minor' prophets

- **Hosea** (750 BC) sees his marriage to an unfaithful wife as a parable of God and Israel. Will the Exile bring the two together again?
- **Joel** (450 BC) preaches a Lenten repentance, and looks for a Pentecostal outpouring of God's Spirit.
- **Amos** (750 BC) foresees the coming Exile as a fitting punishment for Israel's smug self-satisfaction.
- **Obadiah** (600 BC) presents a single chapter on the treachery of Edom during the Fall of Jerusalem.

- **Jonah** (400 BC) is a scathing satire on post-Exile Israel unwilling to share its privileges with the pagan world.
- **Micah** (contemporary with Isaiah 1-39) echoes his call for blind faith in the Saviour to come.
- **Nahum** (600 BC) passionately calls for the destruction of Assyrian Nineveh (compare Jonah above).
- **Habakkuk** (600 BC) is bewildered by a God who sides with Babylon to punish his people. Blind faith is needed (see 2:4).
- **Zephaniah** (600 BC in the midst of the Assyrian invasion) sees hope only in the poor and humble.
- **Haggai** (550 BC) hopes for a new Temple after the return from Exile.
- **Zechariah** (550 BC) echoes these hopes. The last five chapters collect together the later hopes of 300 BC.
- **Malachi** (450 BC) hopes for a new priesthood to replace the apathy of his time.

The Writings

The 20 remaining books of the Old Testament were written (or finalised) too late to be incorporated into The Law or The Prophets, some so late that they were omitted from the Jewish and Christian canon by many, and referred to as *deuterocanonical* ('second list') or *apocryphal* ('unknown author').

Psalms

Most are songs of praise (*Tehillim*), but include all human moods of sorrow and joy. Attributed to David, they have been adapted and added to, to reflect the whole of Israel's history.

As the prayers of Jesus ('My God, my God', 'Into thy hands', etc.), they were naturally adopted by the Christian community, to be prayed *with* him, or even *to* him.

Philosophers

Many psalms question God's strange arrangements for his people, and gave rise to a whole literature exploring the problem of evil:

- **Proverbs** (500 BC, though attributed to Solomon) collects traditional wise sayings (many totally secular) to insist that the wise man (virtuous) is always rewarded.

- **Ecclesiasticus** (200 BC) similarly and rather smugly at greater length.

- **Tobit** (contemporary) uses a story to press home the lesson of virtue rewarded.

But other authors were less optimistic:

- **Job** (500 BC) is an old story in prose (chapters 1-2 and 42), split in half to incorporate 40 chapters of poetry to criticise the glib presumption that virtue is always rewarded. Not in Job's case! The author offers no solution himself, but insists a better one must exist.

- **Ecclesiastes** (200 BC) criticises not only the problem of evil, but the whole problem of life as futile and unsatisfying ('vanity'). Accept what worldly 'rewards' you can, but don't imagine they are the answer.

- **Wisdom** (100 BC) claims to solve the problem of evil by distinguishing between body and soul (with Greek philosophers). *Souls* enjoy their delayed reward in heaven. However, Jewish thought (including the New Testament) demands a heaven with *bodies*!

Religious histories

- **Chronicles/Ezra /Nehemiah** is a rewriting and updating of the Deuteronomic history (Samuel/Kings) by priestly writers about 450 BC, intent on abandoning political aims, and becoming a Church intent only on the worship of God. It is strongly exclusivist.

- **1 Maccabees** (100 BC) tells of the struggle for independence from the Greek Empire.

- **2 Maccabees** (same date) tells colourful stories of this struggle, and breaks through into belief of a life after death (NB: bodily).

Parables

- **Ruth** (like Jonah, 400 BC) protests against Jewish exclusion of foreigners.
- **Judith** and **Esther** (150 BC) use details of past history (Assyrian, Babylonian, Persian) to reassure their readers of Jewish victory over paganism.

Daniel

Like the above, past history (exile in Babylonia 550 BC) is used by a 150 BC author to reassure his Maccabee readers of the victory of the Resistance Movement. Nebuchadnezzar and Balshazzar, etc., are only stand-ins for the Greek Emperor Antiochus Epiphanes.

The 'visions' in chapters 7-12 purport to be prophecies of the future, but are, in fact, statements about present events, heavily disguised. The bestial foreign empires will soon give way to the national and human rule (Son of Man) of a purified Israel.

The New Testament will seize strongly on this title, and award it to Jesus.

Song of Songs – 'the loveliest of all' (400 BC)

A series of love poems attributed to Solomon (patron of 'Wisdom') tell of wooing, home-bringing, union, separation, reunion.

Are these simply a random collection, celebrating human love? Certainly they were (and still are) used as such by Jews.

Or do they form a complex allegory of Israel's relationship with her Husband-God from the Exodus, through the Conquest of Palestine, the Building of the Temple, Babylonian Exile, to the Second Temple? Certainly this is the way Christians have always interpreted the book (cf. John of the Cross, St Teresa, etc.), though some have gone over the top (see Challoner's *Footnotes to the Catholic Douai Bible since 1750).*

Exodus – Covenant – Exile

In any study of the Old Testament it is important to be aware of the three themes that became significant for Christianity.

Exodus

The exodus (escape from Egypt) in the thirteenth century BC was the birth of Israel. A rabble of displaced slaves was turned into a people and a land (see Exodus, Numbers, Joshua).

This basic event was relived symbolically in the liturgy: Passover (*Pesach*), Tabernacles or Tents (*Sukkot*) and Pentecost (*Shevuot*). But also actually in real life: Isaiah 40-55 sees the return from exile as another exodus.

The New Testament will speak of Jesus' death in the same Exodus language (Luke 9:21).

The Old Testament sees the exodus as establishing Israel as God's only son (see Hosea 11 etc.).

But it also asks, 'What about the similarly God-directed exodus of other oppressed peoples? (see Amos 9:7).

Covenant

A covenant is an agreement, contract (testament), or treaty between two parties. Many Old Testament texts emphasise this exclusive bond between God and Israel, suggesting closeness, privilege and superiority (see Genesis 1, 9, 17; Exodus 19-24; Jeremiah 31; Ezekiel 36.)

It is even frequently spoken of as a marriage (see Hosea 1-2; Jeremiah 2-3 and 6-12; Ezekiel 16 and 23).

The New Testament will take up the theme and speak of a new covenant.

But note that even in the Old Testament there is criticism of this exclusive claim (see the books of Ruth and Jonah above).

Is God's one-time contract with the chosen people now revoked, and transferred to Christians?

Or is, perhaps, the whole image expendable, like other institutions that once represented the relationship between God and the world?

Exile

The defeat, first of Northern Israel by Assyria, and then of the Southern Jews by Babylonia in the sixth century BC, resulted in the deportation of thousands. The Northerners never returned.

But for the Jews, the Exile was one of the most creative periods of their history. Stripped of land, temple and king, they turned as never before to God.

The priest, Ezekiel, and the disciples of Isaiah (Deutero-Isaiah) produced some of the Old Testament's finest writing.

See especially the 'impossible' New Temple in Ezekiel 40-48, and the poems of an ideal Israel as God's servant, accepting its suffering and death to save God's world (Isaiah 42, 49, 50 and 53).

The New Testament writers will quote these pieces frequently to describe their experience of Jesus.

Some ideas for discussion groups or essay titles

- Who would you consider to be today's prophets? Why?
- Does 'relativising' the Old Testament make you feel disturbed or relieved? Explain why.
- Is being 'chosen by God' a feather in one's cap, or a frightening burden?
- How do you hold together 'Word of God' and 'words of Men'?
- Explore the theme of covenant (testament) in the Old Testament. Why is it important to Christians?
- Explore the theme of exodus in the Old Testament. In what way did Christianity take up the theme?
- Find examples of some of the literary forms in the Old Testament. How are they to be read today?
- The Old Testament today: in the liturgy, in the home, in school.
- To which strand of the Old Testament (J, E, D, or P) do you warm most? Why?

- How do you reconcile the Genesis accounts of creation with modern science?
- Who was the Suffering Servant of Isaiah 42-53?
- As people of the New Testament, why do we continue to read the Old?
- Muslims insist that only 'the experts' may interpret the apparent contradictions in their Holy Book. Are Christians in the same quandary?

Further reading

A good Bible text with footnotes, such as the *New Jerusalem Bible* (Study edition), Darton, Longman & Todd, 1985. Any good *Concordance* of key words in the Bible will be useful, as will any comprehensive *Bible Dictionary*.

Anderson, B. *Living World of the Old Testament*, Longmans, Green & Co, 1958.

Dale, A. *The Alan Dale Bible (Winding Quest* and *New World)*, Kevin Mayhew, 2002.

Drane, P. *Introduction to the Old Testament*, Lion, 1990.

Richards, H. *ABC of the Bible*, Chapman, 1967.

Richards, H. *Focus on the Bible*, Kevin Mayhew, 1989.

Richards, H. *Plain English Bible*, Kevin Mayhew, 2001.

Richards, H. *The Bible, What Does It Really Say?*, Kevin Mayhew, 1999.

2

The Bible: New Testament

She gave birth to her first son, wrapped him in strips of cloth and laid him in a manger – there was no room for them to stay in the inn.
Luke 2:7

Introduction to the New Testament

The first Christian writings developed in a Jewish world that was beginning to become a Greek world. Without some understanding of this hybrid background, the New Testament will be misunderstood.

The Greek world

Imagine the trauma of leaving one environment and entering another (think of foetuses, teenagers, emigrants, missionaries). Israel experienced this in the exiles of the eighth and sixth centuries BC, but most deeply in becoming part of the Greek (European!) Empire from the fourth century BC.

The Greek mentality

This focuses on the mind and the power of abstract reasoning. What matters are order, precision and exactitude. The ideal person is the scientist.

The Semitic mentality

This focuses on the heart and contemplative reflection. It remains concrete and rooted in life. Jesus was a Semite of the Semites. It was his followers who grew up in a Greek world.

Advantages and disadvantages

Jewish insights, instead of being hived off, began to be shared with the outside world. But there are dangers in over-intellectualising.

The Semitic parable cannot be analysed like a Greek allegory. Existential language means something other when it is understood in purely abstract terms (e.g. 'Son of God'). Christians eventually disowned their Semitic parentage. Is there any way back?

Christian writings

The early Christian writings (apart from a possible earlier version of Matthew and John) became increasingly Greek. Mark's Gospel (AD 65) is so barbaric that the ancients hardly ever quote it. Matthew

(AD 75) is more orderly, but in a repetitious Semitic style, later deliberately diversified by the purely Greek Luke (AD 85). John (AD 100) is so Greek that he adopts Greek philosophy and Gnostic language. Paul (AD 50 – 60) riskily decided that the gospel would only survive if it was cut off from its Semitic roots. How true was this to Jesus?

The writings of Paul

We begin the study of the New Testament with Paul, whose writings are the earliest.

NB: Paul's letters are often off the cuff, not formal, addressed to a readership very different from us (except in sinfulness!); neither are they infallible.

- The communities he writes to (Salonika, Ephesus, Corinth, Rome, etc.) are tiny, smaller even than the Jewish groups, on the fringe.
- Christianity was still seen as a branch of Judaism, still attending synagogues.
- Most were from the lower end of the social scale. See 1 Corinthians 1:26-28, 3:2, 5:11, 6:9-11.
- See 1 Thessalonians 1:8-10, 1 Corinthians 15:3-9, Galatians 2:20-21 for summaries of their faith:

    the repudiation of polytheism for Jewish monotheism

    the centrality of Jesus, Son of God

    his sacrificial death brings history to a close

    his resurrection is the first stage of his return to complete his work, and lead Jews and Gentiles into the presence of God.

1 Thessalonians

This was written about AD 50 to Paul's first converts in Europe who had received him enthusiastically. The whole letter (as also 2 Thessalonians) is about the future Coming of Christ, presumably because of their questions. This is seen as imminent, within a life-time. (Five years later, in 2 Corinthians 4:14, Paul has clearly changed his mind.) These first European converts of Paul were clearly the apple of his eye and his joy (see 1 Thessalonians 2:6-20).

1 Corinthians

Corinth was the meeting point for east to west traffic, and a byword for licentiousness. Two-thirds of the population were slaves (including teachers!). The letter speaks of factions, scrupulosity, superstitions and pentecostalism. Yet this community became a powerhouse of Greek Christianity. The letter suggests that their immorality and individualism stemmed from a Gnostic intellectualism.

Galatians

How exactly should the new 'Christianity' relate to the old Judaism? Is Jesus' teaching in continuity with the Old Testament, or a new departure?

Does being open to the future mean breaking with the past? Paul is convinced that Jesus' insights cannot be contained in the narrow shell of Judaism. He is afraid that contemporary Judaism has lost the emphasis on God's sovereignty. We become good because God is good, not because we are. We do not know whether Paul was successful in Galatia.

Does our present Christianity stem from Jesus, or from Paul? There is danger of absolutising Paul, when it is clear that his theology changed and developed. Yet behind his posturing, there is a moving warmth, and amazing charm.

The good news of the Gospels

When the Gospel is read at Sunday Mass, the sacred book is carried in procession with candles and retinue. It is incensed with alleluias, and greeted like a person: 'Glory to you, Lord', 'Praise to you, Lord'. When the same Gospel is read in a study group, it is handled like any other piece of literature, quite respectfully, but critically. Do these two weekly experiences contradict each other?

The Gospel was preached to arouse faith in Jesus, long before it was ever written down. It is openly propaganda, not history or biography, even after it was put into writing. Written 'preaching aids' (of Jesus' sayings and doings) were eventually strung together, and used in a similar ('synoptic') though distinct manner by Mark, Matthew and Luke.

The first connected piece of writing was the account of Jesus' arrest, passion, death and resurrection – the event that marked him out as the unique Son of God. It is important to read this above all as preaching, not simply history. The resurrection event itself is indescribable and the evangelists exercise considerable freedom in trying to express the inexpressible.

Exercise

Compare the differing stories in Mark 16, Matthew 28, Luke 24, Acts 1, John 20-21 and 1 Corinthians 15, and find some of the inconsistencies: daylight or dark? what witnesses? how many angels and where? joy or fear? how many appearances? in Jerusalem only or in Galilee as well? ascension and sending of the Holy Spirit there and then or later? Never confuse story with history!

Mark's Gospel *c.* AD 65

A close word-by-word comparison with Matthew and Luke will reveal Mark's originality, vividness, breathlessness, colour and clumsiness. His very first chapter uses the word 'and' three times per verse. Luke had to reduce his use of the word 'immediately' from 42 to seven. This Gospel is a haphazard series of images in a pop video.

Not that it is a failed biography. The opening line claims it is a *Gospel*, the good news that Jesus is Son of God. The title is not given again by any human voice until Jesus is dead on the cross. Jesus is a mystery that cannot be solved glibly. Why?

It was written (probably in Rome) in persecution times to warn its readers to expect the same fate as Jesus, who cannot be acknowledged as Son of God until his death on the cross. Even his best friends (see 8:33) could get it wrong.

Paul preached the same message in 2 Corinthians 4:8-11. Turning this theology into a story makes Mark the first Christian dramatist.

Matthew's Gospel *c.* AD 75

In Matthew, Mark's 'heroic leader' becomes 'the Teacher', whose teaching (like Moses') comes in a new *Torah* of five booklets (see 7:28, 11:1, 13:53, 19:1, 26:1) full of Jesus' preaching, beginning (5:1) on the Mount (Sinai). Ostracised by official Judaism, regrouping at Tel Aviv, the followers of Jesus are reassured that the promises of the Jewish Bible have been fulfilled in them (37 times), not in Tel Aviv. Matthew begins and ends his book with the reassurance 'God is with *us*' (1:23, 28:20).

Matthew provides rules and regulations for this 'Church': its members, its missionaries, its mystery (parables), its conduct, and its final vindication. The repetitive style palls for some, but has warmed many through the centuries.

Luke's Gospel *c.* AD 85

Where Mark writes of dying for one's faith, and Matthew of preserving it behind locked doors, Luke writes about living one's faith (41 times 'full of joy') in this ordinary world of men and women. He is the first Christian humanist.

In a world rapidly becoming more and more Greek, Luke imposes *order* (the infancy triptych, the ten-times repeated journey to Jerusalem), *proportion* (Jesus speaks at table not on mountains, and demands compassion not perfection), *openness* (Jesus is descended from Adam not Abraham, is open to Samaritans, is in the company of women and outcasts).

Luke even volunteers a second volume (Acts) where the Good News preached by Jesus continues to be preached by a Church filled with Jesus' Spirit. The story of Jesus is not complete with the telling of his life and death. His community spreads his message and presence to the rest of the world. This volume II is as vivid as volume I, and open-ended to a volume III.

The Gospel of John *c.* AD 100

Of all four evangelists, John is the Eagle, flying high to give an overall view. Browning represents him as saying, 'What first were guessed as points, I now knew stars, and named them' – making explicit the meaning of each tiny detail.

One of John's first stories, the wedding at Cana (2:1-11), bears this out in the symbolism of the third day, glory, hour, woman and wine. Such stories are no longer about who Jesus *was*, but about who Jesus *is* for those who have known him a long time.

This makes John, in one way, the easiest of the four Gospels. Everything is spelled out. Jesus does not say God is a hard task master, so watch it. He says God is love, so go and do likewise. But perhaps this single message needs repeating again and again for it to register.

The first three Gospels all represent Jesus as being secretive about the word 'Messiah-Christ'. John has none of this secrecy: in the very first chapter Jesus is hailed as Messiah, Son of God, King of Israel. Each miracle manifests 'The Glory' (God) because it is a symbol of Jesus' death. Lengthy discourses emphasise this over and over again.

The message of Mark, Matthew, Luke and early Paul that 'the Kingdom is at hand' becomes 'the Kingdom is *now*' (realised eschatology), as any concordance will show under the words 'hour', 'coming', 'glory', 'judgement', 'eternal life', 'resurrection of the dead'. Jesus' last discourse is no longer about a Second Coming, but a coming of Christ into our lives now. Eschatology ('the last things') is not tomorrow, but today.

Miracle stories

- In biblical language, miracles are events (even natural ones), that evoke the God of surprises.
- That Jesus was a healer is incontrovertible. But *all* cultures have had healers, in a religious context *and* outside. They prove nothing.
- Many Gospel texts show Jesus as reluctant to use these powers (cf. the Temptations).

- If readers of the Gospels do not *themselves* feel healed, the accounts are pointless. For John, all the miracle stories are 'signs' of the Cross – the greatest wonder of all.
- Given this slant, it is now impossible to reconstruct 'what really happened'. Only those who experience Jesus doing the same wonders for them, know how true the miracle stories are.

A closer look at two New Testament writings

Revelation

Revelation (Apocalypse) is a style of writing common from 200 BC to AD 100, claiming to 'reveal' the future by accurately 'predicting' events right up until the present.

But the 'predicting' is only a pretence: the authors were actually contemporaries!

Yet the effect of relating past history as if it were future is invigorating: if God won past battles, will he not also be the winner in the end? We see history through God's eyes, not our own, 'reculer pour mieux sauter' (stepping back for a better take-off).

Under a number of different symbols (lion, lamb, Son of Man, horseman) Jesus is pictured as present in contemporary events, and through them winning the victory over the forces of evil (dragon, beast, sea, Babylon).

This victory comes seven times over. Each tableau is complete, and then repeated again and again.

The Church is assured that it wins its victory not in spite of, but in its very suffering. If we find this assurance irrelevant to our lives, are we living too comfortably?

1 Peter

1 Peter comes from the 60s AD, probably from Peter himself. Its theme is as above: in a world not geared for heaven, Christians will have a hard time. To be a Christian is to be a displaced person *(paroikos)*.

The letter illustrates this in *baptismal* terms, and was perhaps originally a sermon for a communal baptism (cf. Exodus theme – lamb, Red Sea, desert, covenant, manna, passover into the Promised Land, Temple of God's indwelling, Eucharist).

The letter stresses the seriousness of Christianity – a hard vocation.

It vetoes digging ourselves in: we are nomads heading for another country! Christianity has today again become a minority, as then.

On the other hand, why should we take so seriously a letter written for a world so different? Vatican II told us to *rejoice* in our world, and not try to escape from it!

- What right have we, as a minority, to condemn the world around us?
- What sense does it make, in our world, to repeat such exclusive language?
- Ought we to be as submissive (e.g. about slavery) as this Epistle suggests? (see 2:13-21).
- How absolute is Scripture?

Some ideas for discussion groups or essay titles

- Which of the four Gospels is your favourite? Why? Read it through and discuss or write your reflections on it.
- Is there any difference between the good news as presented by Jesus, and as preached by Paul?
- Analyse two of the Gospel parables.
- Is 'peace' the word you most associate with Jesus? Why or why not?
- Is the Sermon on the Mount realistic?
- Why does Mark announce Jesus as 'Son of God' on the first page of his Gospel, and then never again till the last page?
- Why is Luke called the 'first humanist'?

- In what way is the Gospel of John different from the other three?
- Find the seven miracle stories in John. Suggest a symbolism in each one.
- Paul has paid a visit to your parish. Compose the letter he later sent to you.

Further reading

A good Bible text with footnotes, such as *New Jerusalem Bible* (Study edition), Darton, Longman & Todd, 1985.

Catechism of the Catholic Church, Chapman, 1994.

Brown, R. *An Introduction to the New Testament*, Doubleday, 1997.

Charpentier, E. *How To Read the New Testament*, SCM Press, 1981.

Dale, A. *The Alan Dale Bible (Winding Quest* and *New World)*, Kevin Mayhew, 2002.

Drane, J. *Introducing the New Testament*, Lion, 1986.

Graffy, A. *Trustworthy and True: the Gospels Beyond 2000*, Columba, 2001.

Grayston, K. *The New Testament, Which Way In?* Darton, Longman & Todd, 2000.

Hooker, M. *Beginnings: Keys that Open the Gospels*, SCM Press, 1997.

Kee, H. and Young, F. *The Living World of the New Testament*, Darton, Longman & Todd, 1960.

Nolan, A. *Jesus before Christianity*, Darton, Longman & Todd, 1977.

Richards, C. *According to Mark*, Blackie/Nelson, 1987.

Richards, C. *According to Matthew*, Blackie/Nelson, 1989.

Richards, C. *According to Luke*, Blackie/Nelson, 1986.

Richards, H. *ABC of the Bible*, Chapman, 1967.

Richards, H. *Focus on the Bible*, Kevin Mayhew, 1989.

Richards, H. *The Gospel According to St Paul*, McCrimmons, 1990.

3

Jesus Christ

At that time Jesus arrived from Galilee and came to John at the Jordan to be baptised by him . . . 'I ought to be baptised by you,' John said, 'and yet you have come to me.'
Matthew 3:13-14

Who was Jesus?

This is the question that Christians (and others) have asked for the last 2000 years. The search into his true identity is called *Christology*. A simple answer to the question goes as follows.

> Jesus was a first-century Jew. His country was under Roman occupation. Jews believed that God had chosen them as a special people. It puzzled them that the Romans had enslaved them. What were the Jews to think? Jesus had a clear answer to that, and he was willing to preach his message fearlessly. He left his carpenter's bench and became a travelling preacher. He talked of his vision of God and of God's loving relationship to people. This vision was to change the course of history.

What was this message that Jesus preached?

Jesus preached about God, as Father. He talked about God's Kingdom or rule over the world. He used stories (parables) to shock his listeners, to make them sit up and think. The theme of all his preaching was freedom – liberation. The Jewish people were hoping for freedom from Roman rule, but Jesus said they really needed freedom from selfishness and sickness of heart and body. He called on them to be compassionate to one another and to forgive one another without conditions attached. He called on everyone to love with the same love that God has for all his people.

What was the result of his preaching?

It seems strange, but as a result of teaching such good news (gospel), Jesus found himself in trouble. His message upset the religious authorities because he quite freely put the spirit of the law before the law itself. He was popular with the crowds, working wonders for them, healing the sick of mind and body. And this didn't help. Jesus was eventually tried by a religious court for blasphemy, and in a secular court for treason against the Roman state. He was executed as a criminal. But, within days, his Jewish followers claimed he was more alive than ever. They spoke out, claiming his presence was among them, and his Spirit in them.

How do we know this?

We know about Jesus from the early writers, Paul, Mark, Matthew, Luke and John (in that order: they wrote between AD 50 and 100). None of them was attempting a biography: the writings were professions of faith in Jesus.

They believed he was sent by God, that he revealed to them what God was really like, and that they could truly call him the Son of God.

Does this answer the question 'Who is Jesus?'

It is not easy to give a clear and adequate answer. Even the Gospels impose limits on us. They describe only the last years of his life (the infancy stories are not straight history), and the writers rarely mention Jesus' motives or describe his state of mind (which makes it difficult to penetrate his inner life). This has led to contemporary theologians asking questions like: How did Jesus understand his own identity? Did he 'discover' his mission as he grew older? Did he think he had a unique relationship to God the Father and Creator? Was he 'born of a virgin' in a biological or symbolic sense?

Christology: three dimensions

- How did Jesus understand his own identity? Who did he think he was?
- How does the Church see Jesus? Divine or human? Or both?
- Who is Jesus Christ for me?

The first two questions do not have straightforward answers. The third question can be answered, but only by each individual Christian. And there will, of course, be many different answers. John O'Grady makes this point in *Contemporary Catholic Theology – A Reader*. He writes:

> Scholastic philosophers often remarked that whatever is perceived is perceived according to the mode of the perceiver. In contemporary language: 'People hear what they want to hear.' Surely this is true

with regard to the present state of Christology, whether the listeners are pope or cardinals or bishops or clergy or religious or laity or even theologians, liberal, centrist or conservative.

Theology is described by St Anselm as faith seeking understanding. This implies that Christian theology has to be continually updated. Theologians have to re-examine fundamental Christian beliefs in order to make the faith more intelligible to their contemporaries. This does not mean that the theologians do not believe in the traditional faith. It means that they take the truth about God very seriously indeed.

Theologians need to examine the past. They have to understand what the words used then meant in that time, and within that culture. They may then use new, contemporary terminology, or put new interpretations on to old ideas. Not all Catholics are aware of this need of research and reinterpretation, in spite of occasional recommendations from Rome for this work to continue.

It should be realised that the great theologians of the past, (Anselm, Thomas Aquinas, Teilhard de Chardin, for example), had their critics too.

Pope John XXIII wrote in 1962:

> The substance of faith is one thing; the way it is presented is another. For the truths preserved in our sacred doctrine can retain the same substance under different forms of expression. *(Documents of Vatican II)*

In 1994 the Pontifical Biblical Commission issued an important document, *The Interpretation of the Bible in the Church*. The authors strongly supported the scholars who search for a new understanding of biblical texts. In the preface, Cardinal Ratzinger wrote:

> The study of the Bible is never finished; each age must in its own way newly seek to understand the sacred books.

Christology is at the heart of this biblical study. In this section we will look at the first of the three questions: How did Jesus understand his own identity?

Who did Jesus think he was?

The popular Webber-Rice rock opera, *Jesus Christ Superstar,* poses an important question in its theme song, namely, did Jesus think that he was who and what people said he was?

The Gospel writers were aware that this was the fundamental question. All four of them present a scene in which Jesus asks, 'Who do people say I am?' And all four Gospels record the disciples as devoutly acknowledging that he is the 'Holy One of God', the 'Christ of God' (see Luke 9:20). Jesus seems to accept the compliment. But are the texts really telling us only who the *authors* thought Jesus was? Would Jesus have agreed with the description of himself? The short answer is that we can't tell.

Clearly the Jesus of history stands behind the Gospel stories about him. But the Jesus of faith has been superimposed on the stories. We, the readers, are looking at a double image. The Gospel writers give us a dozen or more titles to describe Jesus in a way that expressed their own aspirations and convictions. These titles were taken from the Jewish scriptures, because they believed, absolutely, that Jesus was the answer to their age-long prayers. Here are the titles they gave to Jesus.

God

In fact, neither Jesus nor his disciples claimed that he was 'God', full stop. Two obscure texts come near to it (John 20:28 and Hebrews 1:8), and they are both quotes from the Psalms. In biblical usage, 'God' is the title of the Father, of whom Jesus is Son, Word, Servant, Prophet, Chosen, etc. No one has ever claimed that Jesus was God the Father.

If you really loved me, you would be glad that I am going to God, my Father, because the Father is greater than I. (John 14:28)

Lord

The name revealed to Moses at Sinai was 'Yahweh', which means 'He is who he is', that is, the mystery beyond all. Even the name was such a mystery that Jews substituted the word 'Adonai', which is translated as Lord.

The New Testament frequently applies *this* title to Jesus, sometimes clearly in a strong sense, especially after the Resurrection (cf. Luke 1:43, 2:11; John 6:68; Acts 2:36; Philippians 2:9 and Romans 10:9). But in his lifetime? It doesn't look like it. Mark uses it only once. And if it was used more often, we have no way of knowing if it meant anything more than 'Sir'.

Lord, to whom should we go? You have the words of eternal life. (John 6:68)

Word of God

This title is found in John only. It is the title that is based on the Old Testament stories of the Word of God creating all things, calling Abraham and the patriarchs, enshrined in the Laws of Moses, and inspiring the prophets. John sees the long history of the Word coming to a climax in Jesus, in whom we can read God like a book.

In the beginning was the Word, and the Word was with God, and the Word was God. . . . and the Word became flesh. (John 1:1, 14a)

Son of God

Son of God is a metaphor used through the Old Testament for angels, Israel, kings, the virtuous, and any son or daughter of Adam. All these usages entitle Jesus to be called 'Son of God'. In fact, apart from the baptism and Transfiguration scenes, the title is absent from Matthew, Mark and Luke except from the mouth of demoniacs.

In the Profession scene (Matthew 16:16-20) Jesus forbids it, and in his trial *repudiates* it in favour of the title Son of Man (see below). Only the fourth Gospel uses the title (35 times) and Paul copiously (42 times).

It is unlikely that Jesus himself claimed to be *the* only Son of God – a title common at the time for the (political) Messiah.

Jesus' followers happily see him as the model of sonship of God, but they know that they, too, must be conformed to that image (cf. Romans 8:29; Galatians 4:6, 8:29; 1 John 3:1).

To speak of Jesus as 'divine' does not *add* anything to his humanness. He is Son of God by being the *man* he is, in whom we see (undistorted) the face of God.

This is my Son, whom I have chosen: listen to him. (Luke 9:35)

Son of Man

Most scholars agree Jesus used this title of himself: it is only in the Gospels (80 times) and always on Jesus' own lips, not anyone else's. What does it mean?

- In the Psalms, simply *any* human being.

- In Ezekiel (93 times), the fragile and *vulnerable* being that Ezekiel feels himself to be.

- In Daniel 7:13, the *humane* people of God replacing the bestial surrounding empires.

- In the apocalypses (first century BC), an individual *heavenly figure*, scarcely distinct from God.

When the title is applied to Jesus in the New Testament, there are elements of all four meanings, sometimes quite neutrally as in Matthew 16:13, sometimes of Jesus as suffering (Luke 9:58; Mark 14:21), sometimes as a heavenly figure as if of a third party (Luke 12:8).

Clearly, the evangelists capitalised on the ambiguity, after Jesus' death and resurrection. What did the title mean to Jesus? Some scholars think it was deliberately chosen by Jesus to avoid the militaristic overtones of 'Messiah'. Most think that Jesus meant simply 'I' (other rabbis did the same) and that for him it was not a title at all.

. . . Woe to that man who betrays the Son of Man. (Mark 14:21)

Messiah – Christ – Second David

Hebrew *mashiah* means 'anointed' (Greek *Christos*), and was used of prophets, priests and kings. After the demise of the monarchy, it was used of the hoped-for future liberator King (see Jeremiah 30:9; Ezekiel 34:3; Hosea 3:5) and a number of psalms originally written for the king were turned into prayers for the future Messiah (cf. Psalms 2, 72, 110).

The New Testament claims that these hopes were fulfilled in Jesus (see Luke 2:11; John 4:26; Acts and Paul *passim* 400 times).

But Jesus himself seems to repudiate it in Matthew 16:20 and in the trial scenes (see Son of God above).

Did Jesus refuse the title because, before his death and resurrection, it could lead to misunderstanding? Or did he repudiate the title totally as alien to his concept of his mission? In which case, Christians who continue to give him the title are simply saying that there won't be any *other* fulfilment of Old Testament hopes.

(NB Not all Jews continue to hope for a Messiah; the Old Testament has many ways of expressing future hopes.)

Then he warned his disciples not to tell anyone that he was the Christ. (Matthew 16:20)

Suffering Servant

Isaiah 52:13-53:12 speaks of the true Servant of God winning the conversion of a thoughtless world through his suffering and death. The poem probably refers to the persecuted Jews in exile in 500 BC.

The early Christians saw this persecution of the Jews epitomised in Jesus. See (explicitly) Matthew 12:18ff, echoed in Matthew 8:17; Luke 22:37; Acts 8:32; 1 Peter 2:22, etc; see also the title 'Lamb of God'.

According to Mark 10:45 and Luke 24:26, Jesus identified himself with this noble figure, to fulfil the vocation of the whole of Israel. The New Israel would presumably receive the same treatment.

He himself bore our sins in his body on the tree. (1 Peter 2:24)

Saviour

Jesus is given this title in texts such as Luke 2:11; John 4:42; Acts 5:31 and 13:23, and frequently in the New Testament's latest epistles (to counter the emperor cult?).

The metaphor is based on the universal human need for safety and freedom. Many of Israel's judges and kings are given this title, but, basically, the title belongs to God alone (see Luke 1:47 and, strongly, Isaiah 43:11, 45:21). As an image of that saving God, Jesus' ministry is one of rescuing people from their own self-destruction, just like God. And just like all godly people, of course.

Today in the town of David a Saviour has been born to you.
(Luke 2:11)

Holy One of God

In Hebrew, 'holy' means 'separate, other, inspiring awe'. As the 'Holy One of Israel', God is always beyond our grasp. A people that is tied to such a God shares this separateness (see Leviticus 19:2).

As the true Israel, Jesus is naturally given this title in the New Testament (see Luke 1:35; Mark 1:24; John 6:69; Acts 3:14, etc.) and he passes it on to his community.

We believe and know that you are the Holy One of God. (John 6:69)

Chosen, elect

Israel saw itself as chosen graciously out of all nations – with privileges and responsibilities. Only those accepting the responsibilities could be called the true Israel (see Amos 3:2).

The New Testament suggests this 'remnant' is finally fully realised in Jesus alone (Luke 9:35, 23:35).

Yet this title (like the others) is shared by his followers, the New Israel (1 Peter 2:9 etc.).

This is my Son, whom I have chosen; listen to him. (Luke 9:35)

41

Mediator

Two disaffected parties need someone sympathetic to both sides to bring them together. Moses played this role between Israel and God (see Deuteronomy 5:5; Exodus 17:11, etc.), as later did priests, kings, prophets, and the Suffering Servant (see above).

The New Testament calls Jesus the 'Mediator' par excellence (see 1 Timothy 2:5; 2 Corinthians 5:19 and Hebrews *passim*). The emphasis is on Jesus' humanity, representative of all his brothers and sisters.

For there is one mediator between God and men, the man Christ Jesus. (1 Timothy 2:5)

Prophet

A prophet is a spokesman or mouthpiece for God. Inspired means 'breathed into' by God, so that what comes from his mouth is the Word of God. The Old Testament presents Moses as *the* Prophet and promises a replacement when he dies (the Prophets).

When the Israelite monarchy finally failed miserably, many turned this promise into the singular, and looked for the *Prophet* (another Moses), instead of the Messiah (another David).

The New Testament claims this hope was fulfilled in Jesus (see Luke 1:76; John 1:21, 6:14; Acts 3:22 explicitly).

Yet again, this is a title that Jesus shares with his community, all of whom are called to be God's mouthpiece (Acts 2:17).

They began to say: 'Surely this is the Prophet who is to come into the world.' (John 1:21)

Conclusion

It must be asked, in conclusion, how all that has been said in this section ties in with our traditional profession of faith, in which God is a Trinity of Father, Son and Holy Spirit.

The Hebrew Bible speaks neither of a Trinity, nor of a God different from the God of the Gospels. It speaks unswervingly of a

Father, who alone creates, teaches, liberates, loves and dwells with his people Israel, whom he calls to become his Son.

The Gospels present Jesus as this true Israel, who recognises God as his 'Father', and shows the world what it means to be the *Son* of such a God, most clearly in his death.

After his death, Jesus lives on in those who live as he did, and who show themselves to be possessed by the same *Spirit* of sonship that characterised his life.

How does this biblical Christology fit in with the rather more complex official theology of the Church? How does the Church see Jesus?

How does the Church see Jesus? Divine or human, or both?

John O'Grady writes:

> At this point in the history of Christianity people find it acceptable to maintain different models of the Church without detriment to the unity of belief. Believers should also be able to accept a similar position with regard to Jesus. (*Contemporary Catholic Theology: A Reader*)

Are various models of the Church widely accepted today? It is certainly true that theologians who present different 'models' of Jesus are often severely censured. Yet the thinkers in the Church are only doing what their predecessors have done down the ages, namely, trying to present the real Jesus to a contemporary world. Is our real problem to do with the limitations of language?

The early Councils

In the first three centuries, the followers of Jesus struggled to find the right language to profess their faith in Jesus. The biblical titles (as we have seen) gave them their clues, but not everyone accepted the interpretation given by early theologians and teachers. Meetings (Councils) were called to sift the opinions being offered. Those discarded by the bishops were called 'heresies'.

A 'trinitarian' (three-in-one) theology resulted. It was expressed in highly technical terminology. All Christians claimed that Jesus was more than merely a prophet of God: he was the final clue to the meaning of the word 'God', and he had to be included in the definition of God. Further, though he was no longer present with them in a bodily way, he continued to be with them 'in the Spirit'. How can this 'threeness' be reconciled with the 'oneness' of God so strongly defended by all Jews, including Jesus?

- In the second century, the *Gnostic* heresy undermined the humanity of Jesus by claiming that Jesus was really a divine being disguised as a man. This is also known as *Docetism* (Greek *dokein* – to seem).

- The priest, *Arius*, protested that Jesus was only a human being. This was condemned at the *Council of Nicaea* in AD 325. The Nicene Creed ruled that Jesus was of the same substance as God the Father.

- A century later, the bishop *Nestorius* argued against this wording, and denied that Jesus had a divine nature. He claimed that Jesus was two persons – Mary being the mother of the human person, not mother of God. This was condemned at the *Council of Ephesus* in AD 431.

- To counteract Nestorius, *Eutyches* insisted that Jesus was so much one person that he had only one nature, a divine one. His followers were condemned at the *Council of Chalcedon* in AD 451. The Council introduced the technical language of a 'two nature-one person' model. Jesus was presented as true God and true man: the eternal Son of God incarnate ('made flesh').

Many today find the technical language of 'substance', 'nature' and 'person' confusing. The Chalcedon formulation is so complicated that it is difficult to see how it ever answered the question: 'Who is Jesus?'

> We are all agreed in teaching . . . one and the same Christ, the Son, the Lord, only begotten, in two natures unconfused, unchangeable, undivided, inseparable. The difference of natures will never be abolished by their being united but rather the properties of each

44

remain unimpaired, both coming together in one person and substance, not parted or divided among two persons but in one and the same only begotten Son, the divine Word, the Lord Jesus. *(Enchiridion Symbolorum, Denzinger 148)*

The tortured language indicates the difficulty of finding words to describe the mystery of God and his relationship with human beings through the life, death and resurrection of Jesus. It is perhaps not surprising that Christians hover between opposing 'heresies'! Some want a divine Christ; others need a human Christ. There will always be a tension between the two.

Perhaps it would help to consider two different ways in which theologians are talking today. The *two-world theology* can be described in a simple way as follows: there are two worlds, one of God up there, the other of human beings down here. God is the transcendent Father who created the world. In his omnipotence he can alter the rules if he so wills. We have glimpses of God, especially in the person of Jesus, because he was sent down by God to us. Jesus is divine because he is God's own Son. He has a foot in both worlds. Everything on earth is a distraction and only temporary. People should live their lives with one eye on heaven where the Trinity dwells. True riches are in heaven, and the poor and suffering will only be comforted when they die – providing they have lived good lives. The reward is eternal happiness.

The *one-world view* approaches God from the opposite end. All that can be known of God is known through human experience. God, the reality behind all creation, is best understood in terms of love. That love, God himself, is most clearly seen in the human Jesus. The compassion, love and forgiveness he showed were unique, and lead Christians to call him the very Son of God. God, the Creator-Father, who made people 'in his own image', is actually limited by his creation. People have free will to use their gifts for good or evil, and God will not intervene to change his laws. There is only one world, God's world, and people are called to make it grow towards its perfection. Injustice, poverty and greed distort God's plan and prevent people from seeing God in this world of his.

These two theologies are literally worlds apart. Probably neither gives an accurate picture of the actual relationship between God and Jesus. The two-world theology is characteristic of thinking passed down from the scholastic middle ages. Some suspect that it harbours the Docetic heresy that denied Jesus humanity. The one-world theology (inspired and developed by the Liberation Theologians in the Third World) so emphasises the humanity of Jesus that some suspect it harbours the Arian heresy which questioned Jesus' divinity.

Would it be sensible to accept a certain plurality in Christology? No one model will satisfy, because all models used in theology are incomplete. Each model is developed as a result of historical circumstances, and makes most sense when seen in context. The one-world view (above), for example, emerged from the experience of faith in Latin America, where injustice and poverty inspired the model of Jesus as liberator.

Who is Jesus for me?

The doctrinal formulas that try to analyse the substance, nature and person of Jesus are not particularly helpful to the ordinary Christian who wants, quite simply, to follow the Jesus of the Gospels. Christians are those who have found the life and teaching of Jesus an inspiration for their own lives. Of course, they believe that Jesus is more than an inspiring figure to imitate. They accept him into their lives as the Son of God, and they celebrate his life and follow his teaching by being members of the Church with all its traditions, customs and beliefs.

Christians believe in the resurrection of Jesus. One aspect of the resurrection is the continued presence of Christ in the world, in the lives of ordinary people. Jesus lives on in those who try to imitate his life and base their ideals on his teaching. Sometimes ordinary people act with a love, compassion and forgiveness that seem beyond the humanly possible. These extraordinary Christians have often been deeply influenced by one or other aspect of Jesus' life or teaching of the Gospel.

Think about these examples:

- *Jesus took Peter, John and James with him and went up a hill to pray.* (Luke 9:28)
  Benedict, Teresa of Avila and Julian of Norwich centred their lives on *prayer*.
- *Go and sell all you have . . . give to the poor . . . then come follow me.* (Mark 10:21)
  Francis of Assisi, William Booth and Charles de Foucauld welcomed *poverty*.
- *Jesus healed many who were sick with all kind of diseases.* (Mark 1:34)
  Vincent de Paul, Mother Teresa and Cicely Saunders were inspired *to heal* others.
- *Go then to all peoples everywhere and make them my disciples.* (Matthew 18:19)
  Thomas Aquinas, Dominic and Wesley spread the good news as *teachers/preachers*.
- *Do for others just what you want them to do for you.* (Luke 6:31)
  Martin Luther King, Julian Filochowski and Sr Ita Ford chose to work for *human rights*.
- *Love your enemies and pray for those who persecute you.* (Matthew 5:44)
  Maximilian Kolbe and Mary McAleese chose *reconciliation* as the way to live.
- *Whoever does not carry his own cross . . . cannot be my disciple.* (Luke 14:27)
  Stephen, Thérèse of Lisieux and Oscar Romero embraced *the cross* with love.
- *Forgive them Father! They don't know what they are doing.* (Luke 23:34)
  Elizabeth Fry, Desmond Tutu and Sr Helen Prejean put *compassion and forgiveness* first.

What aspect of Jesus' life and teaching inspires you most, and leads you to action?

47

Some ideas for discussion groups or essay titles

- 'The Jesus of history stands behind the Gospel stories about him. But it is the Jesus of faith that has been superimposed on the stories.'

  What does this mean? Give examples from the Gospels to illustrate your answer.

- Analyse the titles *Son of God* and *Son of Man*. Did Jesus see himself as either or both?

- In what way did Jesus see himself as Messiah? Or did he?

- To what extent do the Councils of Nicaea, Ephesus and Chalcedon clarify for you who Jesus is?

- In what way can Jesus be called *Liberator*? What does he liberate us from, and why?

- Choose an outstanding Christian (saint?) and show how in their life they made Jesus present to the world.

- Do you find any evidence that the risen Jesus is present with us today?

Further reading

O'Grady, J. *Models of Jesus Revisited*, Paulist Press, 1997.
Kelly, J. N. D. *Early Christian Doctrines*, Black, 1985.
Richards, H. *Jesus: who did he think he was?*, Kevin Mayhew, 2000.

4

The Church

The Church is the Body of Christ . . . In the unity of this Body, there is a diversity of members and functions. All members are linked to one another, especially to those who are suffering, to the poor and persecuted.
Catechism of the Catholic Church, 805-806

Introduction to the Church

The great anomaly of Christianity is that only through institution can the message of a non-institutional Jesus be preserved. (Raymond Brown, *The Churches the Apostles Left Behind*)

If you stop people in the street and ask them what they understand by the term 'Church', answers will be quite varied: large buildings, Christian groups, the Mystical Body of Christ, the People of God, the community, a large authoritarian institution. How do *you* see the Church?

Hans Küng wrote a major work on the nature of the Church (see bibliography). His preface makes the comment that 'One can only know what the Church should be now if one also knows what the Church was originally.' So what was it originally? Hubert Richards gave a definition in his *ABC of the Bible*:

> The Church is nothing other than the community of those to whom the risen Christ has given his very Spirit, and who in that Spirit form the very Body of Christ.

Richards, as a biblical scholar, is using the imagery first used by St Paul in his letter to the Romans:

> *Just as each one of us has one body with many members, and these members do not all have the same function, so in Christ we who are many form one body, and each member belongs to all the others.* (Romans 12; see also 1 Corinthians 12)

Our concept of the Church is influenced by the form that the Church takes at any time. Küng warns us, 'All too easily the Church can become a prisoner of the image it has made for itself at one particular period in history.' Today, for example, people could be excused for regarding the Church as a sign of disunity, with denominations never in total agreement with one another, sometimes even in open violence against each other. On the other hand, the Church today is often one of the few voices raised for the poor.

Every age has its own image of the Church. These images arise out of particular historical situations and the reactions of the theologians of the day. But at the same time there is a constant, unchanging factor in the changing images. We can call this the *essence* of the Church, which is drawn from its origins in New Testament times. Throughout this chapter we will look at both the essence and the images.

Church History

Origins of the Church prior to AD 100

The New Testament does not lay down a doctrine of the Church to be worked out in practice over the centuries. It starts with the Church as reality, a happening, an historical event. The reflection and the theology came later. It is called *ecclesiology*.

- The Church's origin lies in the life of Jesus Christ and his teaching.
- It is built on the faith of the Apostles who carried on this teaching. *I tell you that you are Peter, and on this rock I will build my church.* (Matthew 16:18.)
- There are already different images of the future Church in the New Testament: the Pauline epistles suggest a charismatic Church, while the Acts of the Apostles and Pastoral letters offer an image of order and office (see the Council of Jerusalem in Acts 15).

The Patristic period *c.* AD 100-1200

This is the age of the Church Fathers.

- The early thinkers, St Ignatius of Antioch (died *c.*107) and St Irenaeus (died *c.*200) were not so much concerned with the Church, but with God and Christ. They wrote to defend Christianity against heresy. Creeds were not yet written; belief was expressed in the liturgy, celebrated by bishops.
- The image of the Church in the first three centuries was influenced by the hostile pagan state in which it grew up. Hippolytus (*Apostolic Tradition c.*215) saw the Roman Empire as a satanic

51

imitation of God's Kingdom. Subsequently, harmony between the established Church and the Christian empire provided a new image. Eusebius (died 340) saw the Roman Empire as divinely ordained to prepare for Christianity, with the emperor as the defender of the Church.

• The earliest Church Councils were concerned to refute heresies about the nature of Jesus in relation to the Father. Creeds were formulated.

325 Council of Nicaea. Athanasius of Alexandria. Nicene Creed.
381 First Council of Constantinople. Basil of Caesarea.
431 Council of Ephesus. Cyril of Alexandria.
451 Council of Chalcedon. Leo of Rome.

'I believe' (*Apostles Creed*) is the faith of the Church professed personally by each believer, principally during Baptism. 'We believe' (*Nicene Creed*) is the faith of the Church confessed by the bishops assembled in council or more generally by the liturgical assembly of believers (*Catechism of the Catholic Church* 167).

Note that in this *Patristic* period the Eucharist makes the Church. The Eucharist was the *Mystical Body* of Christ. The bishop celebrated this mystery, and the community (local churches) formed the *Real Body* of Christ in the liturgical celebration. A dramatic change of emphasis and interpretation came during the next period of the Church's history – the *Scholastic* Period. This is illustrated below.

Patristic model   **Scholastic model**

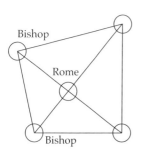

	Patristic	Scholastic
Real Body	Church	Eucharist
Mystical Body	Eucharist	Church

*c.*1200

The Scholastic period *c.* AD 1200-1900

This is the age of the Schoolmen, based on a fascination with logic and a return to Aristotle. The shift away from biblical theology was accompanied by a gradual shift in location – from the monastery to the university.

Great changes took place in the government of the Church and in the development of doctrine, especially of the Eucharist. The close partnership between Church and State gave enormous power to the Pope and bishops.

- Pope Gregory VII (died 1085) was called the 'Vicar (stand-in) of Peter'.
- Pope Innocent III (died 1216) called himself the 'Vicar of Christ'.

The shift in thinking is significant.

The Patristic age came to an end with eleventh century theologians like Berengar (died 1088) and St Anselm (died 1109). Berengar was excommunicated because he opposed the idea of transubstantiation. (It was discussed at the Fourth Lateran Council in 1215 but only became a doctrine of faith at the Council of Trent in 1551.) Theological debate was heightened in the eleventh century by the rivalry that existed between the East and West. Rome and Constantinople disagreed with each other over primacy, and broke from each other in 1054.

Pope Innocent III's pontificate (1198-1216) is regarded as the culminating point of both temporal and spiritual supremacy of the Roman See. All states came under his power. He sent Crusades to reclaim Jerusalem from the Muslims and burnt Constantinople to the ground. But his zeal also gave him the insight to promote two great spiritual movements led by Francis of Assisi and Dominic Guzman.

The Dominican Order produced *St Thomas Aquinas* (died 1274), the greatest thinker and writer of the Middle Ages. His influence and intellectual authority has dominated Roman Catholic doctrine ever since.

The fourteenth and fifteenth centuries saw growing unrest against the power of Rome and its many corrupt practices. This led to the *Reformation* and further splits amongst Christians. The Roman Catholic Church recognised these events as a clear call to put its own house in order – the *Counter-Reformation*.

The Council of Trent (1545-1563) produced a host of theological statements specifically framed to combat 'Protestant' theology.

The First Vatican Council (1869-1870) met in the midst of turmoil in Europe. It was never completed and left an unfinished top-heavy definition of the Church. (The Second Vatican Council's task was to put right this imbalance). The Scholastic period really came to an end as the nineteenth century drew to a close.

To sum up: In the *Scholastic* period understanding of the Eucharist was reversed. In the *Patristic* period the Eucharist makes the Church. In the *Scholastic* period the Church makes the Eucharist. The Fathers said the Church was the *Real Body* of Christ and the Eucharist was the *Mystical Body*. The Scholars reversed this. The Eucharist, which had been a mystery to fathom became a miracle to believe. Theologians today point out that the laity was diminished by this theology. It was expected to stop thinking.

Modern Age (1900 onwards)

All too easily the Church can become a prisoner of the image it has made for itself at a particular period of history. (Hans Küng, *The Church.*)

Vatican I was called to free the Church from the 'prison' of the scholastic image. Vatican II was needed because the first Council had left a distorted image. In the years between the two Councils, attempts were made to initiate new thinking, and to ask new questions. Biblical, liturgical and catechetical movements were started. Then came Pope John XXIII who was not afraid to want a modern Church. He said: 'The substance of the ancient deposit of faith is one thing, the way in which it is presented is another.'

Vatican II (1962-1965)

The original intention was to present Church teaching in 70 documents. In fact only 16 were produced. The most important were the four Constitutions:

- Constitution on the Sacred Liturgy (*Sacrosanctum Concilium*)
- Dogmatic Constitution on the Church (*Lumen Gentium*)
- Dogmatic Constitution on Divine Revelation (*Dei Verbum*)
- Pastoral Constitution on the Church in the World of Today (*Gaudium et Spes*).

The other documents were called simply Decrees or Declarations.

It is essential for theology students to read these documents. As a guide, *To Live Is To Change* is highly recommended as a starter (see 'Further reading', page 67).

Lumen Gentium: Constitution on the Church

This is probably the most important and influential document produced by the Council. Most time was devoted to it during the Council, and it reflects some dramatic changes in the thinking of the bishops. It falls into eight sections:

- The Mystery of the Church
- The People of God
- The Hierarchical Constitution of the Church
- The Laity
- The Universal Call to Holiness in the Church
- Religious Life
- The Eschatological Character of the Pilgrim Church
- The Blessed Virgin Mary.

The document moves away from the negative scholastic theology that had rejected real and perceived heresies. *Lumen Gentium* is a positive text woven from the Bible, the Fathers and human experience. One contemporary issue was sadly totally overlooked – the role of women in the Church. The document explores the nature of the Church, without asking questions or seeking answers. This is left to the Pastoral Constitution *Gaudium et Spes*.

Eight Decrees issued by the Council are practical applications of *Lumen Gentium*. They look at the role of the laity, bishops, priests and religious (see below). They also address the issues of missionary activity (see p. 61ff) ecumenism and relationship with the Eastern Catholic Churches (see p. 65ff).

Lumen Gentium opens up – though it does not resolve – the complex issues of authority in the Church and the role of priesthood.

Organisation of the Church Community

As the followers of Jesus grew in great numbers, the question of organisation became crucial. How should Christians maintain unity with each other and with the past? If disputes arose, who settled them? Who had the last word? Christian denominations have approached this from different angles. The Roman Catholic Church claims to have kept close to the New Testament pattern of organisation.

The laity

Cardinal Newman was asked by a priest, 'Who are the laity?' He replied, 'The Church would look foolish without them.' When the Middle Ages identified the Church with the clergy, lay people felt increasingly treated as second-class citizens. The Church structure became triangular, with the Pope at the top and laity flattened at the base. Vatican II encouraged a rethink: the laity *are* the Church, the followers of Christ.

Several of the Council documents (especially *Gaudium et Spes*) looked at the world people live in as the arena of the lay apostolate. The Council emphasised the 'universal call to holiness' (*Lumen Gentium*, Chapter 5) and this led Council theologians to provide a basic theology of the lay apostolate, in a decree called *Apostolicam Actuositatem*. The groundwork had already been done during the twentieth century as social change, the development of education and the advance of technology demanded a Christian response.

The Church expanded at the same time as the vocation to priesthood declined. Involvement of the laity became a necessity, and theologians like Yves Congar OP began to set the role of the laity on a theological and scriptural basis.

Each one, as a good manager of God's different gifts, must use for the good of others the special gift he has received from God. (1 Peter 4:10)

Since the Council, it is recognised that the document on the laity was limited in some respects and even inconsistent. It was a document of its time. Even so, lay people are today involved in parish, deanery and diocesan pastoral councils. They train as catechists, youth leaders and lay chaplains; they teach in seminaries and work alongside the clergy in many areas of Catholic life.

Bishops

In the New Testament, leadership was exercised by 'overseers' (*episkopoi*) and 'elders' (*presbyteroi*). It is unclear whether these roles were different but, by the second century, the *episkopos* was accepted as the single leader of the Christian community in a given place. He celebrated the Eucharist for his community. The way a bishop was elected changed over the centuries. In modern times he is chosen by the Pope to take care of a diocese – the local group of Catholics.

The Vatican II decree, *Christus Dominus,* defined the role of bishops in the Church. The document clarified the relationship between local bishops and the Pope. There had been a long power struggle between bishops and the Vatican Curia in the past. Vatican I worked out a theology of the Pope who, with his Roman Curia, exercises authority over the universal Church. Vatican II confirmed this theology strongly by giving considerable attention to bishops, and developed a theology of the Episcopal College. This envisaged a more shared leadership of the Church, with bishops governing, teaching and having liturgical authority in their own dioceses. The Council speaks of bishops as 'servants of the community . . . Good Shepherds . . . true fathers who manifest a spirit of love and care for all.'

After the Council, Pope Paul VI set up a Synod of Bishops, a consultative body of bishops, which meets in Rome every three years. National Bishops' Conferences have been established to express the unity of local Catholic Churches. Our National Conference of Bishops has given strength to the Catholic presence in England and Wales, by addressing both the Catholic community and the nation on controversial and pastoral issues. The bishops gained great respect for their reflections on political and social issues in the document *The Common Good* (1996).

Priests

The bishop, as a successor of the Apostles, accepts the fullness of ordination. Priests are 'ordained' (formally commissioned) to assist the bishop in the ministry of the word and sacrament. Priests take care of parishes and other communities. Vatican II produced two decrees on the priesthood: the documents, *Optatam Totius* and *Presbyterorum Ordinis*, considered the formation, ministry and life of priests. They attempted to redefine the role of the priest and give him a training more suitable for the modern world, based firmly on the gospel and a life of service and prayer.

The new vision given by the Council was quite radical. Priesthood was seen as much more than a life based on the liturgy and Church law. A priest's life should be modelled on the Gospel and concerned for the human person. Many new ideas in formation and priestly life were introduced, taking into account the human needs of the individual and his need for support. The way was left open for dialogue with Protestant Churches on ministry, and pastoral initiatives, such as priest-workers, were undertaken.

The two Council documents, written hurriedly, failed to reflect on the often lonely and difficult life that a priest can encounter. Dioceses have taken various steps to overcome this problem and National Conferences of Priests have been set up. There is no doubt that the priesthood is in some crisis today, with unsolved problems of celibacy, declining numbers, and an unclear relationship with the role of the laity.

Deacons

In the New Testament, a deacon (*diakonos*) is someone who 'serves'. All followers of Christ were expected to do this, but there is some indication (Philippians 1:1; 1 Timothy 3:8-13; Romans 16:1) that it was highlighted in an ordained ministry. Since Vatican II this office has been revived. Married men may be ordained as deacons. Their numbers are on the increase in many dioceses. Some bishops and priests are unclear about the role they should play in the parishes. In some cases the deacon is given only pastoral duties, which could be performed by the laity of the parish. The interaction of ordained and lay partnerships in the Church is still in a state of development.

Pope John Paul II pointed out, in 1990, that clergy and laity have the same mission:

> People today put more trust in witnesses than in teachers, in experience than in teaching, and in life and action than in theories. The witness of a Christian life is the first and irreplaceable form of mission: Christ, whose mission we continue, is the 'witness' *par excellence* and the model of all Christian witness. (*Redemptoris Missio*)

Service of others – the Church's mission

> The vocation of humanity is to show forth the image of God and to be transformed into the image of the Father's only Son. (*Catechism of the Catholic Church* 1897)

> Charity is the greatest social commandment. It respects others and their rights. It requires the practice of justice, and it alone makes us capable of it. Charity inspires a life of self-giving. (*Catechism of the Catholic Church* 1889)

At the heart of Catholic social teaching is the conviction that each person is unique, and created in the image of God. The Catechism says: 'The dignity of the human person requires the pursuit of the common good. Everyone should be concerned to create and support institutions that improve the conditions of human life' (no. 1926).

The Catechism goes on to stress that service of others is most urgent 'when it involves the disadvantaged, in whatever area this may be.' This is, of course, based on the example of Jesus, especially as shown in the Gospel of Luke.

Throughout the Church's history, it is evident that 'service of others' has been a common denominator. The monasteries, from earliest foundations, were the schools and local medical centres. In every century there have been outstanding Christians who dedicate their lives to the poor and disadvantaged. Many active religious orders and congregations were founded in the eighteenth and nineteenth centuries, to combat the poverty and injustices caused by changing social patterns (especially the Industrial Revolution in Northern Europe).

Missionaries have, over the centuries, not only spread the news of a spiritual Kingdom of God, but have brought education, health care and land reform to countless underprivileged societies. It was their experience that led bishops in the developing world to insist that the Church make a definitive 'Option for the Poor', in 1968. The bishops of England and Wales had already invited their people to respond to disadvantaged peoples in the developing world, and set up the Catholic Fund for Overseas Development (CAFOD) in 1962.

At home there are numerous organisations, many working in local parishes, trying to address the needs of communities and individuals. The diocesan year books give details: children's societies, child protection groups, pastoral services for the deaf and hearing impaired, St Vincent de Paul Society, Justice and Peace Commission, Commission for Welfare of Refugees, etc. These and other groups are under the direction of the *Diocesan Commissions for Social Concern*.

However, the Catholic Church's social doctrine and teaching has been called its 'best kept secret'. In some ways there is a great gap between the Church's social teaching (impressively outlined since the late nineteenth century in papal encyclicals and in the Vatican II document, *Gaudium et Spes*) and the lived reality of Church life.

Further reading

Linken, I. *Back to Basics – Revisiting Catholic Social Teaching*, CIIR, 1994.

Encyclicals:

- *Rerum Novarum*, Pope Leo XIII, 1891.
- *Quadragesimo Anno*, Pope Pius XI, 1931.
- *Mater et Magistra; Pacem in Terris*, Pope John XXIII, 1961, 1963.
- *Populorum Progressio; Octogesima Adveniens*, Pope Paul VI, 1967, 1971.
- *Redemptor Hominis*, Pope John Paul II, 1979, etc.

The Church – a new model?

The model of the Church bequeathed us by the Council of Trent was of a hierarchical Church . . . a pyramidical structure with the Pope at its peak. At the base were the laity, the recipients of authority which always passed from top to bottom. At the Second Vatican Council (1963-5) the world's bishops rejected this model. There had been a change of thinking going on in the Church, from conceiving herself as a hierarchical society to seeing herself as a COMMUNITY; from a pyramid to a circle. (Adrian Smith, *Tomorrow's Parish*, 1983)

In the 1960s, new thinking about the Church came from countries (especially in South and Central America) exhausted by poverty and injustice. *The Movement for Basic Christian Communities* evolved in Brazil, and this led to the Vatican II bishops calling for a return to the early practice of forming 'Church' around small lay communities. A nun who witnessed the development of these communities wrote:

What we see in Latin America is a new model of the Church. Don't fall into the error of thinking there is now a new popular Church in Latin America. There isn't. What we have found is the Christian Church founded by Christ, but it is a new way of being that Church in the World. (Sister Pamela Hussey, HCJ, *In Touch*)

This new model for the Church arose out of a different way of looking at God's relationship to people. It is called *Liberation Theology*, which can be described as the attempt to practise faith in situations that are politically, economically and socially unjust. This challenges Christians. It demands action for change. Its aim is the ultimate liberation of both rich and poor.

The determined move to readjust human values, in the light of the Gospel, made a decisive impact on the whole Church when the Latin American bishops met in Medellin, Colombia, in 1968. They committed the Church to work for the liberation of the people from violence, poverty and injustice. This 'option for the poor' was renewed at Puebla in 1979. Other Christian denominations joined the movement and produced the *Kairos Statement* of 1985. It may be significant that whilst the Christian Church in Europe is rapidly losing its voice and influence, the same cannot be said for Catholic Christianity in the Third World.

This movement away from the triangular structure of the Church has not been universally welcomed by members of the hierarchy and the laity. A leading Liberation theologian, Gustavo Gutierrez, said that the poverty of the poor was not simply an occasion for acts of generosity, but rather a compelling obligation to an entirely different social order. Some in the Church have regarded this as far too political and radical. Others, who embraced the challenge, died for it. Archbishop Oscar Romero, six Jesuit priests, several nuns and many lay people in El Salvador, witnessed to their heroic faith by losing their lives in defence of the poor. Today it is the Colombian Catholics who are dying for their support of human and religious rights. Almost weekly, priests are shot whilst saying Mass, or bombs are thrown into churches.

When criticized for being 'dangerously on the left', Fr Jon Sobrino, a Jesuit priest in El Salvador, said that the Church and the Jesuits 'have made an option for the poor'. This is the option Jesus made and it is also the option of prophets like Isaiah and Micah. That doesn't make the Church Communist; it simply makes the Church Christian.

Obviously such a revolutionary new understanding of the Church is not to everyone's liking. It upsets so many of the priorities we once automatically took for granted that it is bound to be resented by many. But it deserves serious consideration, as does any new model that is based on an honest attempt to live the Gospel.

The Catholic's relationship with other Christians and with world religions

On 21 November 1964, the Second Vatican Council issued a Decree on Ecumenism (*Unitatis Redintegratio*). It was to become one of the most important Council statements. Ecumenism is the desire to bring all Christians (indeed all people) into unity, the unity for which Jesus prayed: '*May they all be one . . .*' (John 17:21).

Previously the Catholic Church had developed an ecclesiology that presumed that the fullness of the Christian faith could be found only in the Church of Rome. Other Christian denominations had begun to face the scandal of rivalry between missionary groups and, in 1948, had founded the World Council of Churches. But the Catholic Church steadfastly distanced itself from this movement, and repeated statements from Rome in 1832, 1854, 1863, 1864 and 1927 explicitly forbade any Catholic participation in ecumenism. 'The claim that the way to eternal salvation may be found in any religion whatever is impious and destructive . . . No one can be saved outside the apostolic and Roman Church.' (Pius IX, 1854)

Many older Catholics will recall that, until the 1960s, they were forbidden to attend funerals and other services in non-Catholic churches, and even to pray with other Christians.

Vatican II brought about an enormous change by declaring ecumenism to be the work of the Holy Spirit. How was this about-turn to be negotiated? Bishop Butler wrote:

> The problem, and it is not an easy one, is, granted this unchanged and unchangeable Catholic position, how to make Catholic participation in the Ecumenical Movement not just an exercise in Christian courtesy, but a positive and constructive contribution. (*The Theology of Vatican II*, Darton, Longman & Todd, 1981)

What sort of contributions have been made over recent years? Two strongly contrasting positions have been taken up.

The hard line

Some would wish to continue taking a hard line, charitably, of course, but unyieldingly. The Christian message is a collection of revealed truths, and all that true Christians can do is to preserve them intact, like a curator. Since the truths are eternal, fixed and unchangeable, people will either accept them or not, but there is no question of the truths themselves undergoing any change. We may wish to brush these truths up from time to time, to ensure that they mean the same today as they did yesterday. We may try to present them in a more attractive packaging, but that is peripheral, a matter for the media experts, the icing on the cake. The real job for Christians is to pass these truths on from one generation to the next, with the words, 'Come and share the treasure which I possess, because there is no truth or salvation outside of that.' Jesus' words were explicit: 'No one can come to the Father except through me. Go and teach all nations, everyone everywhere, and get them to possess these truths as you possess them, otherwise they are lost.'

> We should praise God that people want to return to a universal union. We Catholics enjoy that unity, and we should pray for those deprived of it, and urge on them their duty to seek for it, for it is they who defected from it. The truth is one and indivisible. There are no fundamental and non-fundamental parts of the faith. We offer it to others for their acceptance in its entirety. It is a trust given to us by God, which we must keep intact and hand on intact. The idea of touching it up is as unthinkable as trying to bring an Old Master up to date. The Church already *is* one. We rejoice that others desire that oneness. We praise all the truths that they already profess. We try to explain gently and humbly the truths they do not yet see. And we pray for them. (Bernard Leeming, SJ, in *The Catholic Gazette*)

The previous paragraph was written in 1956, well before the Vatican Council. But it represents a view about non-Catholics and non-Christians still common in the Catholic Church. There are even official Roman documents that can be quoted to support it. For example:

> It is true that followers of other religions can receive divine grace. But it is also certain that, objectively speaking, they are in a gravely deficient situation in comparison with those who, in the Church, have the fullness of the means of salvation. (*Dominus Jesus* 22, 2000)

> The [Catholic] Church cannot forgo her missionary activity in the world, namely to announce that it is in Christ, the Way, Truth and Life, that people find salvation. (*Novo Millennio* 56, 2001)

Another approach

Yet there are other official Roman documents that take a less rigid line, and no longer express the Christian message as a collection of truths of which Roman Catholics have a monopoly, but as a contribution towards genuine dialogue with other world religions, with no hidden agenda in the background. As early as 1964, the Vatican Council declared:

> Those who, through no fault of their own, do not know the Gospel of Christ, yet nevertheless seek God with a sincere heart, and try to do his will as they know it, may achieve eternal salvation. [Salvation is possible] even for those who have no explicit knowledge of God but strive to lead a good life. (*Lumen Gentium* 16)

Pope John Paul II has from time to time expressed himself in similar conciliatory terms:

> The documents of Vatican II see various religions as so many reflections of the truth. The routes taken may be different, but there is a single goal, a single quest for God and for the full meaning of human life. (*Redemptor Hominis* 11, 1979)

> Dialogue is the opposite of trying to impose our views on others. Dialogue means listening respectfully to others, trying to discern all that is good and holy in each other's beliefs, and co-operating in everything that favours mutual understanding. (*Jerusalem*, 2000)

These quotations are no longer couched in missionary and conversionist terms, but in a spirit of ecumenism, where the aim is no longer for one party to convert the other, but for both parties to understand each other in order to convert whatever needs converting in themselves.

In this spirit, many Catholics today no longer express the Christian message as a collection of truths of which they have the monopoly, but as a vision of God through the eyes of Christ. The Christian is called to treasure everything that is Christlike, for that is true God-liness. Wherever there is love, said one of Jesus' first disciples, God is there. All those who live in love, live in God, and God lives in them, whether they call themselves Christians, or Muslims, or atheists. The Great Commission to go and teach everyone should not be allowed to sabotage the Great Commandment, which is to go and love them.

Where next?

Which of these two approaches should today's Catholics take to promote the unity that Christ prayed for? The harder, or the softer line? Or should one perhaps take both, the missionary and the openly ecumenical approach, as the occasion demands? Is the first *too* hard, and liable to repel others rather than attract them? Is the second *too* soft, and too dismissive of Christianity's most central doctrines? The search continues.

Some ideas for discussion groups or essay titles

- Examine the different models of the Church. Assess your parish against them. What models operate in your parish?

- It is a generation since the Second Vatican Council. What has been the effect of the Council on the Church?

- Choose one specific area of Church history and examine its importance for the development of the Church.

- 'There was no conflict in the early Church.' Is this true? What criteria are used to determine orthodoxy?

- Write a critique of either *Lumen Gentium* or *Gaudium et Spes*.
- What is Liberation Theology? Why has it not been received enthusiastically by some of the hierarchy and the laity? How do you view it?

Further reading

Catechism of the Catholic Church, Chapman, 1994.

Catholic Bishops' Conference of England and Wales, *Interfaith Dialogue*, Catholic Communications Service, 2002.

Flannery, A. (ed.), *The Documents of Vatican II*, Dominican Publications, 1966.

Hayes, M. and Gearon, L. (eds), *Contemporary Catholic Theology: A Reader*, Gracewing, 2001.

Jamison C., Lundy D., and Poole M. *To Live Is To Change*, Rejoice Publications, 1995.

McBrien, R. P. *Catholicism* (new edition), HarperCollins, 1994.

5

The Sacraments

In Baptism we have been called to form one body.
The Eucharist fulfils this call.
Catechism of the Catholic Church, 1396

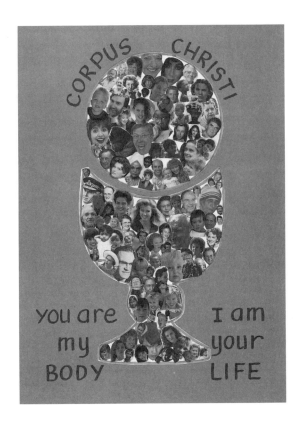

Introduction

A Catholic poet, Gerard Manley Hopkins, wrote that 'the world is charged' with the grandeur of God and that it will 'flame out', like shining from shook foil ('God's Grandeur').

The psalmist had expressed the same wonder:

The heavens declare the glory of God. (Psalm 19)

The two poets were men of faith who looked through the finite into the infinite. They saw in the ordinary secular world glimpses of the sacred. Poets and people with faith use a language of 'symbol' to try to express what they see with insight rather than with ordinary sight. Fr Hugh Lavery, saddened at the growing loss of religious faith in the Western world, described it in the following way:

> The disease of the Western world is an eye-disease, an astigmatism which has narrowed vision, so that people only see things as surface. (H. Lavery, *Sacraments*)

God is a mystery beyond all mysteries. Religious people seek words and ideas that might express something of that mystery. They use signs and symbols, things that can be 'touched', to remind them of the transcendent God who cannot be touched.

Of all the Christians who have recognised the symbolic power of the world, St Francis of Assisi is the best known. In his *Canticle of the Sun,* he rejoiced that the created world and everything in it constantly reminded him of the wonder of God himself. Being the poet and prophet he was, rocks reminded him of that 'rock who was Christ', spring lambs symbolised the Lamb of God, lights represented the Light of the World, and trees became a symbol of the Cross.

This sacramental view of the world is not peculiar to Christians. It was, for example, strongly apparent in the native American tribes. It is an embarrassing fact that Christianity sent missionaries to convert these 'pagans' without any inclination to listen respectfully to their cultural wisdom and search for truth.

> When we see changes of day and night, the sun, the moon, and the stars in the sky, and the changing seasons upon the earth, with their

ripening fruits, we realise that it is the work of someone more powerful than ourselves.
(Chased-by-Bears, Yanktonai Sioux, *Native American Wisdom*)

Jesus, the Sacrament of God's Presence

In Jesus, we are able to know God in human terms; that is what it means when we say that Jesus is the Sacrament of God's Presence. (P. Wilkinson, *Focus on the Sacraments*)

For Christians, the word 'God' cannot be used on its own. Since the birth of Jesus it will always have overtones of the man in whose life the one God was embodied (incarnation). Jesus' life was unique. It reflected in every way the love, compassion and forgiveness of God. And this has to be the starting point for all Christian understanding of the sacraments. Paul had put it in these words:

He is the image of the unseen God. (Colossians 1:15-16)

and John expressed it in this way:

Jesus said, '. . . he who has seen me has seen the Father.' (John 14:9)

John's Gospel is a good starting point for a Christian understanding of sacrament. John used the imagery of the vine. A single life force flows through the vine and its branches. *I am the vine and you are the branches. He who abides in me, and I in him, he it is who bears much fruit, for apart from me you can do nothing* (John 15:4-5). Christ is continually creating the Church by feeding his life and spirit into it.

Indeed, the Church has always understood that it was born in the moment of Jesus' death. John wrote: '*When they came to Jesus, they found him already dead, and so instead of breaking his legs one of the soldiers pierced his side with a lance and immediately there came out blood and water*' (John 19:33). The two principal sacraments of the Church (and the only ones recognised by the Protestant and Free

71

Churches), Baptism and Eucharist, are understood to be symbolised by the water and blood which came from Jesus' side.

As well as John, Paul also used symbolism that has been adopted by the whole Christian community. For him, the resurrection of Jesus meant that his living presence was now to be found in his followers. For this reason he spoke of the Church as the Body of Christ. The Church locates Jesus, the Christ, in space and time. Just as the body communicates the spiritual dimension of our personality, so the Church has to be the 'face of Christ', revealing to the world who and what the risen Christ is. The Church is called to be a tangible expression of the vision and purposes of the risen Christ in all the circumstances of time and place in which it finds itself.

This understanding of the Church has led theologians to describe the Church itself as a 'sacrament'. The Vatican Council put this into words:

> By virtue of its relation to Christ, the Church is a kind of sacrament of intimate communion with God and of the unity of all mankind. That is, she is a sign and instrument of such union and unity. (*Lumen Gentium* 1)

A sacrament requires a sign that is visible, observable by human beings. In other words, it is the responsibility of the Church to give tangible evidence of the new way of being human that was shown in the human Jesus – a way of love, compassion and forgiveness.

Sacraments and sacramentals

During the Patristic Age the word 'sacrament' meant anything that signified a Christian mystery. Augustine said a sacrament was 'a sign of something sacred'. Any ecclesiastical ritual or the symbolic elements within them were called sacraments. It wasn't until the Middle Ages that the Scholastics distinguished *seven sacraments* from *sacramentals*. The latter are described as: 'Blessings, prayers or sacred objects designated as sacred in a unique way by the Church.'

The traditional definition for sacrament is 'an outward sign of inward grace'. A more recent definition calls sacraments 'significant actions which transform humans by bringing them into contact with the saving grace of Jesus Christ'.

A sacrament has the following characteristics:

- it is a sacred and symbolic action
- it consists in an intimate encounter with Christ
- it comes to us from Christ and is celebrated through the Church
- it recalls the past, brings it into the present, and gives hope for the future.

What does all this mean in everyday language and experience?

Human beings always need to find meaning in their experiences. In this way they discover themselves as they are, and have insights into who they might become. Our key life experiences are the most obvious times when we attach meaning to our lives. Birth, death, friendship, falling in love, work, failure, ill health or success, are the key experiences that

> can break suddenly into the daily routine of life to challenge the meanings we thought explained ourselves, open up new possibilities and add depth to our vision of life . . . This way of reflecting on experience and interpreting it is sacramental, that is, it calls up and makes present, in and through itself, something that is beyond itself. (Maurice Lynch, *Course Notes for CCRS Course*)

In ordinary language, the sacraments are celebrations of life's meaning, seen with the eyes of Christ. Life is God's greatest gift, and through the sacraments Christians celebrate all that this implies.

- **Baptism**: the celebration of human life, both in the family and in the community.
- **Confirmation**: the celebration of the presence of Jesus in the world, through his Spirit of love.
- **Eucharist**: the celebration of Christ's continuing presence in the world, as the One who sustains us.
- **Reconciliation**: the celebration of God's infinite compassion and love which is expressed in his prodigal forgiveness.

- **Marriage**: the celebration of human love and relationships as an image of divine Love.
- **Orders**: the celebration of a vocation to offer service to the community.
- **Anointing of the sick**: the celebration of the compassion for the sick and the healing that so strongly characterised the life of Jesus.

Sacraments of initiation – Baptism, Confirmation and Eucharist

Baptism

Baptism is the celebration of human life, both in the immediate family and in the wider community. It is the sacrament of solemn initiation into membership of the Christian family.

Background

In the Old Testament, membership of God's family was expressed in the covenant that God graciously made with his people. The acceptance of this *covenant* was expressed in circumcision, which even infants could receive.

In New Testament times, this mark of belonging to God's people was reinforced by a *baptism* in water. This was a ritual for adults (unlike circumcision), available to pagans as well as Jews, symbolising (positively) an entry into the coming Kingdom of God, and (negatively) a painful exodus from past attachments: in short, a birth and a death.

The New Testament presents John the Baptist as one of the leaders of this radical movement, and Jesus as such an enthusiastic candidate that he and his disciples eventually themselves became baptisers (John 3:22). Both the joyful and the sorrowful aspects of this ministry are stressed: *This is my beloved Son,* (Matthew 3:17 etc.); *There is a baptism I must still receive, and how great is my distress till it is over,* (Luke 12:50).

The baptised Christian is invited to die with Christ and enter into his risen life. The symbolism of water expresses this. The *catechumen* (person to be baptised) enters the water to die to everything that is not of God's Kingdom and rises out of the water to a new, trans-formed and converted life. It is a radical invitation and more appropriate for an adult's response than for that of an infant.

Over the first three centuries a rite of initiation, the *catechumenate*, developed, which was a three-year preparation for adults. The bishop baptised those who were 'elected', on Easter night. By the fourth century this pattern had broken down because the number of baptised grew too large. Infant baptism became part of the pattern.

By the fifth century, when infant baptism had become the norm, fundamental changes were made to the rite itself. The ceremony became more private, and the theology shifted from a positive invitation to live a renewed life in Christ, to a negative preoccupation with Original Sin. By the fourteenth century the baptismal ceremony disappeared from the Easter ceremony altogether. Baptism became just a simple part of Christian life, and the rites were reduced to a minimum. The radical conversion call of the Gospel was lost.

Vatican II and renewal

The Council steered thinking back to the early Church, and moved the emphasis away from individual salvation from original sin, to initiation into a community that tries to make the 'Kingdom of God' a reality. This Kingdom is a community of love, forgiveness, justice and compassion. The baptismal rite recognises the individual's need to renounce sin, but speaks of original sin as the condition of a wounded, broken and rebellious human world. The invitation to the catechumen is to make the Kingdom of God a reality. It is a radical challenge.

The RCIA

The Rite of Christian Initiation of Adults was introduced in 1972 and is now practised in many parishes. It is a renewal of the ancient catechumenate preparation of would-be converts into the Catholic

Church. It is a shared journey for adults, and takes place within the local Catholic community. During the Easter Vigil the 'elect' are admitted into the Church by the three sacraments of initiation: Baptism, Confirmation and Eucharist.

Confirmation

Confirmation is the celebration of the presence of Jesus in the world, through his Spirit of love.

The sacrament is traditionally described as the sacrament of the Spirit, and those preparing for the sacrament have a wealth of biblical material to explore:

• the creative Spirit of God (Genesis 2:7)

• the prophetic Spirit of God (Exodus 19:18; 1 Kings 19:9-13)

• the Spirit of Jesus (Luke 1:35; 4:18-19)

• the Spirit of Pentecost (Acts 2:1-4)

• experiencing the Spirit (Acts 4:31; 1 Corinthians 1:4-8; Romans 8:15-16).

In the first centuries there was only one rite of initiation – Baptism. By the fourth century, the increased number of candidates meant that new members were baptised together at Easter or Pentecost. When the bishop was available to visit a local church, he gave a second anointing, 'confirming' the first. This gradually became the sacrament of Confirmation. Clearly, the two sacraments should be seen together. When infant Baptism became the norm it was sensible to have a 'confirmation' of baptismal promises at a much later date. This should remind Christians that the sacrament of Baptism was only the beginning of a journey in faith.

Yet there remain divided views about the 'right' age for Confirmation. Good arguments can be made to support a variety of pastoral approaches. In the spirit of the Second Vatican Council, the return to a catechumenate has indicated that the three sacraments (Baptism, Confirmation and Eucharist) should be considered together as the initiation rite into the community of the Church. The Orthodox Church has always kept this practice:

The essential rite of Confirmation is anointing the forehead of the baptised with sacred chrism, together with the laying on of the minister's hand and the words, 'Be sealed with the Gift of the Holy Spirit' in the Roman rite, or 'The seal of the Gift that is the Holy Spirit' in the Byzantine rite.

When Confirmation is celebrated separately from Baptism, its connection with Baptism is expressed, among other ways, by the renewal of baptismal promises. The celebration of Confirmation during the Eucharist helps underline the unity of the sacraments of Christian initiation. (*Catechism of the Catholic Church* 1320, 1321)

Eucharist

The Eucharist is the joyful celebration of Christ's continuing presence in the world, as the One who sustains us.

At the Last Supper, Jesus links the two elemental sources of new life, bread and the body. The community of the Church comes into being and receives ongoing life through the giving of bread become body. (Maurice Lynch, *Course Notes for CCRS Course*)

The sacrament of the Eucharist is at the heart of the Church, the body of Christ. The Christian Church came into being when, following Jesus' death and resurrection, those who believed in him came together to celebrate his new presence in the sharing of bread and wine.

On the same night that he was betrayed, the Lord Jesus took some bread and thanked God for it and broke it, and he said, 'This is my body which is for you; do this as a memory of me.' In the same way he took the cup after supper, and said, 'This cup is the new covenant in my blood. Whenever you drink it, do this as a memorial of me.' (1 Corinthians 11:23-25)

When a Christian community gathers for Eucharistic worship:

• **they celebrate a common memory**
The Last Supper was the Passover, when the Jewish people celebrated their deliverance from slavery and the covenant that God made with them. By celebrating this memory they brought the

reality into the present. Jesus told his friends that their Passover must be in memory of him.

- **they celebrate a common ritual meal**
  The Last Supper was anticipated by many meals that Jesus shared with friends, outcasts and sinners. Meals involve giving and sharing: the meals Jesus shared symbolised his compassion and concern for everyone. No one was excluded from his table.

- **they celebrate a common sacrifice and are transformed**
  At the Last Supper Jesus indicated how his love would reach its fulfilment in his death. Paul was quick to recognise that the community was called to share in the sacrifice of Christ. *Is not the bread we break a sharing in the Body of Christ? Because the loaf of bread is one, we, many though we are, are one body, for we all partake of one loaf* (1 Corinthians 10:16-17). Paul saw his ministry as linked to this sacrifice: *In my own flesh, I fill up what is lacking in the sufferings of Christ for the sake of the Body, the Church'* (Colossians 1:24).

The first Christians, sharing in the consecrated bread and wine, discovered the presence of Christ in a particularly intense way. Theologians and Councils over the centuries have sought to find a language that accurately expresses the reality. Sadly, this sacrament of unity has been a constant cause of disunity, from the eleventh century Berengar of Tours (who believed only in a 'spiritual' presence of Christ in the Eucharist), to the recent ARCIC deliberations between Catholics and Anglicans. Some theologians suggest that the Scholastics muddied the waters. In the early Church, the Fathers saw the Eucharist as the Mystical Body of Christ and the community as the Real Body of Christ. The scholars of the Middle Ages reversed this. The Eucharist became the actual Body of Christ, a miracle to believe, instead of a mystery to fathom.

Sacraments of healing – Penance and Anointing of the sick

Penance and Reconciliation

The sacrament of Reconciliation is the celebration of God's infinite compassion and love, expressed in his prodigal forgiveness.

Forgiveness of sin is a key Christian doctrine, which lies at the heart of the Gospel. Jesus preached consistently that sinners were as welcome in the Kingdom of God as saints. This becomes clear by imagining the different ways God might react to sin:

(a) by exploding with anger and telling the sinner that he had gone too far: 'Get out of my sight !'

(b) by a controlled anger: telling the sinner that such wrongdoing demanded some kind of compensation

(c) by a great generosity and forgiveness, with one condition – that the sinner make amends and promises not to sin again

(d) by an overgenerous (prodigal) forgiveness where God says to the sinner, 'I love you so much I can forgive everything. Come and be close to me, I've forgotten your sins already.'

Which of these four reflect the good news of the Gospel?

The Catholic Church has been accused of fostering a sense of guilt in its members by the practice of 'confession', which seemed to concentrate on the seriousness of sin rather than on the over-whelming graciousness of God. One priest puts it this way:

> The sacrament of Confession, in the experience of many people, had belonged to a spirituality which reflected an obsession with sin and a sense of being overwhelmed with guilt. It encouraged within people a very poor self-image, with little experience of forgiveness and a sense of being accepted. (Peter Wilkinson, *Focus on the Sacraments*)

The sacrament of Penance was in danger of being reduced to a frequent routine, where penitents (sinners) listed their sins, anony-mously, to a priest. He gave words of encouragement, granted a penance in compensation, asked the penitent to make an act of contrition (which included the promise not to sin again) and then gave absolution (forgiveness). Some Catholics are still happy with this system, but it has declined dramatically in recent years.

It would be wrong to suppose this means people have lost their sense of sin. It may indicate that they are aware of sinfulness in a deeper sense. The traditional style of confession presumes that God acts as in (c) above. Many biblical theologians don't recognise that God in the Gospels. They point out that his forgiveness is without conditions (read *The Prodigal Son*, Luke 15:11ff).

Since the Vatican Council, the Church has reflected on another aspect of sin – its communal nature. Many Christians today see *original sin* as an image of the sinful world situation into which we are born. This shift in emphasis brought about a change in the name of the sacrament, from *Penance* to *Reconciliation*. A Synod of bishops was called in 1983 to discuss 'Reconciliation and Penance in the Mission of the Church'. The discussions produced a fine balance between reflections on personal sin and 'social sin'. Archbishop Worlock asked for less emphasis on personal failings and more on a search for social justice, and asked Catholics to reflect on their responsibility to help create a just, honest, equal and peaceful world.

Anointing the sick

Go back and tell John what you are hearing and seeing: the blind see, the lame walk, those who suffer from dreaded skin diseases are made clean, the deaf hear, the dead are brought back to life, and the Good News is preached to the poor. (Matthew 11:4-6)

The Gospels are full of stories about Jesus healing the sick and comforting sinners. It features strongly throughout his ministry. It was the evidence he himself pointed to, to show that the Kingdom of God is here and now, in this life, whenever compassion and love are shown. Christians have always tried to imitate this care of Jesus for the sick and the dying. The sacrament of Anointing of the Sick is the Church's way of responding to his example. Jesus was eager for his disciples to heal the sick as he did:

*And these signs shall follow them that believe . . . They shall lay
their hands upon the sick and they shall recover.* (Mark 16:17-18)

History of the sacrament

It is clear that, from the earliest days of the Church, the disciples
took Jesus seriously. James wrote:

*If one of you is ill, he should send for the elders of the church, and
they must anoint him with oil in the name of the Lord and pray over
him. The prayer of faith will save the sick man and the Lord will raise
him up again; and if he has committed any sins, he will be forgiven.*
(James 5:14-15)

For the first 800 years there were no formal rituals: the people simply
took oil to their bishop, who blessed it saying, 'May it give strength
to all who taste it and strength to all who use it.' For the next 300
years, until AD 1150, the priest took over the role of anointing the
sick before they confessed their sins at the point of death. The
forgiveness of sin became the focus of the practice. The five senses
were anointed, with the words: 'Through this holy anointing (and
God's blessing) may the Lord forgive you whatever sins you have
committed by the sense of . . .'

The scholastics of the Middle Ages tended to translate all the
traditional practices of their day into dogmatic principles. In AD 1150
the condition for receiving the sacrament became danger of death,
and it could only be received once. The effect of the sacrament was
essentially the forgiveness of sins, to prepare the penitent for entry
into eternal life. It became known as *Extreme Unction.* Surprisingly,
the *Council of Trent* did not accept the narrow discipline of the
scholastics, and recognised that the sacrament could bring about
bodily healing. But it was not until Vatican II that we were reminded
that it was more appropriate to call the sacrament the 'anointing of
the sick'.

A *New Rite of Pastoral Care of the Sick* was introduced in 1983,
which made it clear that the ministry of the sick is the responsibility
of everyone. The purpose of the sacrament is to comfort the sick,

help them trust in God and give them strength to overcome their anxiety about death. It is to help the sick and dying to experience the compassion of Christ.

The Sacraments at the Service of Community

The Catechism states that 'the sacraments of Holy Orders and Matrimony are directed towards the salvation of others . . . through service to others' (1534). All the baptised are consecrated to a common priesthood, which means that *all* Catholics are called to ministry, with equal rights and obligations – both men and women. 'The essential task of this ministry is to enable the many varied gifts of the Spirit to flourish within the community and so build up the body of Christ.'

Holy Orders

In the chapter on the Church, we looked at the special ministry of service that belongs to the ordained clergy – bishops, priests and deacons, (see pages 57-59). The Second Vatican Council became aware that the priest's role is one of 'daily increasing difficulty in the renewal of the Church', not least because, over the centuries, the clergy were seen as separate from and superior to 'lay people'. This attitude has been difficult to shake off, although great efforts have been made to do so.

The Church has always maintained that through baptism *all* the faithful share in the common priesthood of Christ. Some members of the Church choose to participate in a particular way in the mission of Christ. Theirs is a ministry

> conferred by the Sacrament of Holy Orders, where the task is to serve in the name and in the person of Christ the Head in the midst of the community. (*Catechism of the Catholic Church 1591*)

This priestly vocation is a formal commission by the Church for the ministry of word and sacrament. Priests work with the bishop by taking care of parishes and other communities. The importance of an ordained ministry in the Church is expressed in the Catechism (no. 1593) in these words:

> The ministries conferred by ordination are irreplaceable for the organic structure of the Church: without the bishop, presbyters and deacons, one cannot speak of the Church. [Cf. St Ignatius of Antioch, *The Epistle to the Trallians, Ad Trall* 3:1]

A few years ago, Monsignor Anthony Philpot addressed the bishops of the United Kingdom whilst they were on retreat in Rome. His words were a striking call for hope and confidence in the future at a time of doubt and darkness. He began his address:

> Catholic clergy in Britain have a sense of crisis and a feeling of guilt. No wonder. We are the generation of priests and bishops who have lived across the watershed from boom to decline. We have presided over what, in statistical terms, is a reversal in the Church's fortunes.

Fr Philpot outlined the model of the Catholic Church in the 1950s, pointing out that it was materialistic, self-satisfied, rather preoccupied with its own history and nationality, and it was 'very, very clerical'. It was hardly surprising that radical changes had to come. He invited the clergy to believe that the Church, which was undergoing a crucifixion now, would rise again but in a new form. 'The Church will be purified, by God's unmerited kindness, from much of the baggage which has encumbered it in our lifetime.'

The words he addressed to the bishops at the end of the talk would benefit the whole Catholic community. He advised the Church leaders to look at Christ as the model:

> We must concentrate on him, not on theories or ideologies. Leadership and perfecting of faith depend on him, not on the frenzied activity of priests or bishops, rushing about like hamsters on a treadmill.

There is clearly a need for deep reflection and debate on the very nature of ordained ministry. It will be enriched if supported by a sensitive and patient laity.

Marriage

The laity has its own crisis to confront, in an age when relationships and marriages are weakened by contemporary social behaviour. In a newspaper article on marriage one 16-year-old commented: 'I used to think marriage was something celebrities did before they got divorced.' Students questioned about marriage said that they only knew what they had gleaned from television soaps and celebrity gossip in the tabloids. Posh and Becks were their role model married couple.

It is an interesting commentary on the Second Vatican Council that there is no Decree on married life. Marriage and family are mentioned, almost by the way, in the Decree on the Apostolate of the Laity. There is a short chapter on marriage in the second part of the *Constitution on the Church Today*, under the title 'Some problems of special urgency'. Damian Lundy summarises the chapter as follows:

> In the chapter on family life, mutual love between partners and raising children are both affirmed as the aims of marriage, but the whole tone is one of affirming and celebrating the fulfilment of the whole person through married life, not just raising children. (Jamison, Lundy and Poole, *To Live Is To Change*)

This represents a remarkable move forwards. Traditional Catholic teaching on sexuality had been legalistic, sin-centred and rested heavily on the thought of Augustine of Hippo (AD 354-430), who saw human sexuality after the Fall in an almost totally negative light, as dominated by lust. For him the only moral purpose of intercourse was procreation. The Church adopted this thinking up until the Second Vatican Council. The Council avoided the traditional language of 'primary and secondary ends of marriage', and left the way open for a more positive understanding of human sexuality.

All Christian denominations teach that marriage is a serious life-long commitment. The love that husbands, wives, parents and children have for each other is an image of God's love. It also reflects the union of Christ with the Church. Marriage is celebrated as a sacrament in the Catholic Church. ('Christ the Lord raised marriage between the baptised to the dignity of a sacrament', *Catechism of the Catholic Church*, 1660.) The couple exchange marriage vows to one another in a religious service, often during the celebration of Nuptial Mass. In this way, they administer the sacrament to one another. Marriage is a difficult vocation, and the couple seek strength from God. The priest gives his blessing on behalf of the Church:

> You have declared your consent before the Church. May the Lord in his goodness strengthen your consent and fill you with his blessings. What God has joined together let no man put asunder.

It is understandable that the young people interviewed about marriage (see the beginning of this section) had no strong desire for a church wedding. Marriage today presents a crisis in the Church. This is the problem:

- Serious lapse of adults, as well as youth, from parish communities
- Society's weakening attitude towards lifelong commitments
- Disenchantment of married couples about Church teaching on contraception
- Growing numbers of divorced and separated Catholics
- Young people most likely to live with partners before, instead of after marriage.

There is clearly a need for deep reflection and debate on the nature and responsibility of married and family life. It will be enriched if supported by a sensitive and patient clergy.

Some ideas for discussion groups or essay titles

- Explore the meaning of signs and symbols, especially as adopted by the Church.
- Explore how the seven sacraments can be seen as a celebration of life. Do they always feel like celebrations?

- What is the relationship between Baptism and Confirmation? How has the Church expressed this relationship over the centuries?
- The sacrament of the Eucharist is the sacrament of unity, yet is sometimes the occasion of disunity. Explain this and suggest some solutions.
- Trace the historical development of the sacrament of Penance/Reconciliation. How has the emphasis shifted, especially recently?
- It is said that there is a crisis in the priesthood today. Why is this so? Is there a solution?
- It is said that there is a crisis in married life today. Why is this so? Is there a solution?
- How are young people prepared for the sacraments in your parish or school? Have you any ideas to offer your community?

Further reading

Catechism of the Catholic Church, Chapman, 1994.

Jamison, C., Lundy, D. and Poole, L. *To Live Is To Change*, Rejoice Publications, 1994.

Hayes, M. and Gearon, L. *Contemporary Catholic Theology: A Reader*, Gracewing, 2001.

Wilkinson, P. *Focus on the Sacraments*, Kevin Mayhew, 1987.

6

Christian Morality

What am I going to do?
What should I do?

Introduction

The Church claims that we can understand what God is like. Jesus has revealed this to us in his life, death and resurrection. We therefore know what we should be like, in order to find lasting peace and happiness. The Church also believes that Jesus taught us how we should live our lives day by day. Living out our Christian beliefs as they affect our decision-making is called *morality*.

Morality is distinguishing between right and wrong. The Catholic Church speaks out boldly, saying 'This is good . . . this is bad'. Many people, Catholics included, criticise the Church for taking a hard line on moral issues, especially on sexual and medical matters. However, others praise the Church for her courage in speaking out with conviction. Recently Pope John Paul II was nominated by the international news magazine, *TIME*, as their 'Man of the Year'. *TIME* said that in a year when many lamented the decline in moral values or made excuses for bad behaviour, Pope John Paul II resolutely set forth his vision of 'the good life' and urged the world to follow it.

The language of moral theology

We need to distinguish between *religion* and *revelation*. 'Religion' is the human effort made to reach out in order to 'touch' the transcendent (God). 'Revelation' denotes the initiative taken by God to reach out towards his creation. Christianity is first and foremost a *revelation*.

Theology is the science of re-articulating this revealed Good News for successive generations. It is 'faith seeking understanding'. The content of revealed truth is explained in *dogmatic theology*. The meaning of revealed truth is examined in *systematic theology*. Moral theology or Christian ethics is part of systematic theology.

Both the Greek *ethos* and the Latin *mores* mean 'what is characteristic or customary'. In the actual use of the words, *ethics* has come to mean the characteristic way one behaves to fit into an orderly society. *Morality* refers to the objective rightness of the actions people perform. The distinction between the two is thin.

How do people make moral decisions? From the moment we are born we begin to learn how to behave in society, and we are influenced by our family, our neighbourhood, our schooling, our choice of friends, the media and our religious beliefs. Moral questions can be baffling. Is it always wrong to steal? What if you are starving? Was the Christian, Bonhoeffer, right to have plotted to kill Hitler? People will give different answers, some with great passion, even though they cannot give reasons for their point of view. Christians, however, believe that good guidance is available for the task. God has made known his will in a number of ways:

- The Bible
- The life and teaching of Christ
- The teaching of the Church
- The inspiration of the Holy Spirit
- Actions undertaken in love
- One's conscience.

Christian moral behaviour depends on the relative authority given to these, and to the way they are interpreted. On many issues there is one Christian voice. But there are some areas of disagreement because Churches and individuals interpret 'authority' in different ways. The Catholic Church emphasises loyalty to the authoritative moral code developed over the years, based on Scripture, Church tradition, and the official *magisterium*.

The 'magisterium' is normally used of the bishops exercising their official role as teachers of the Catholic faith. This day-to-day teaching is called the 'ordinary magisterium'. It becomes 'extra-ordinary' when they solemnly gather together in council (as they did at Vatican II in 1963-65) in order to discuss and formulate what Catholic Christians believe; or when the Pope speaks on behalf of his brother bishops solemnly and explicitly to define a point of faith or morals. In such rare cases, Catholics believe, the providence of

God will continue to preserve the Church from error in handing on the revealed Word of God.

In order to explore the Catholic Church's position on morality we need to understand the basic language of ethics used by moralists in general:

- Moral judgements about rightness and wrongness fall into two categories, teleological and deontological.

  Teleological judgements are based entirely on the end results of an action (*telos* is a Greek word meaning 'end'), e.g. 'It would be morally wrong for me to tell the truth because it could cause the death of someone.'

  Deontological judgements are based on a set of rules that must be obeyed (*deon* is a Greek word meaning 'must'). Acts are right or wrong in themselves, not because of the end result. 'I'll tell the truth even though it means that man will be free to kill again.'

- In making ethical judgements *conscience* is always involved.

- Goodness, according to the philosopher Aristotle, is something that fulfils its purpose.

  This idea was explored by St Thomas Aquinas in the *Natural Law* theory which is the basis of Roman Catholic moral teaching. Whatever frustrates a natural purpose is wrong. Right action is what fulfils a natural purpose.

- Goodness comes from God and is revealed by him. Good actions are those that conform to his will.

The Catholic position on morality has been re-emphasised in recent years. Firstly, the Pope issued an encyclical letter, *Veritatis Splendor* (1993) in which he warns Catholics to be wary of moral decisions based on teleological grounds. The end does *not* justify the means. He also reinforced the Church's official disapproval of two moral systems preferred by many people today, *utilitarianism* and *situation ethics*.

Utilitarianism is the system developed by British-born Jeremy Bentham and John Stuart Mill in the eighteenth century. They claimed that 'the greatest good of the greatest number' is the best rule to be taken when making moral decisions.

Situation ethics. Forty years ago the Protestant theologian Joseph Fletcher wrote that moral decisions should be based on the general principle of love, not on rules. He felt that this was closer to the Gospel. He claimed that no rule can be absolute, and that each situation had to be judged for itself, on the basis of love (in the demanding, self-sacrificing, biblical sense of *agape*).

Secondly, the recently published *Catechism of the Catholic Church* (1994), devotes its third section to the moral life of the Christian as essentially a *participation in the life of Christ*. Fr Kevin Dring, a moral theologian, has summarised the importance of the Catechism as follows:

> In the Catechism as a whole, there exists a strong internal cohesion whereby the person of Jesus Christ is central. More than this, however, the truths expounded throughout flow out of one central truth: the trinitarian life of God into which all are drawn and which itself flows into our lives and our world. This theme, the 'economy of salvation', forms the backbone of all the teaching contained in the Catechism: believing, worship, the sacraments, the moral life, and prayer. The Catechism is not an end in itself but must rather be situated within its proper context: the ongoing renewal of the whole life of the Church begun in the Second Vatican Council. It cannot be simply read as an academic work but must, to quote the Bishop's Conference of England and Wales, be read 'with the eyes of faith, seeking to go beyond the words which are always inadequate to the truths they seek to convey'. (Fr Kevin Dring, in a lecture to permanent deacons in training, Wonersh, 2002)

The Catechism clearly defines the post-Vatican II position on moral theology. It is a system slowly developed over the centuries.

Brief history of Catholic moral theology

The Early Fathers (second to sixth century)

They followed no systematised moral teaching. Their writings, in response to the threat of pagan culture, attempted to encourage

Christians to walk in 'the Way of Light' and to recognise 'good' as 'seeds of Christ'. Moral formation was really a part of the process of Christian initiation. *St Augustine* (d. 430) is recognised as the first systematic moral theologian. He preached and wrote about natural and divine law and most aspects of behaviour, both individual and collective. In *The Confessions* he analysed the disposition of the sinner. However, his ideas inclined to be negative (especially his restrictive ideas on sexuality) and this influenced the development of Catholic morality until the present day.

Celtic monks and penitentials (seventh to tenth century)

Over these three centuries the monks developed an unhealthy focus on *sin*. The sacrament of Confession was developed at this time, copying the daily practices of monks confessing their faults to the abbot. A pre-arranged amount of penance, or a tariff, was attached to every sin. The practice was associated with spiritual direction; this provided a means of moral education.

Scholastic period (eleventh to twelfth century)

The Franciscan, Bonaventure (who followed Plato), and the Dominican, Thomas Aquinas (who followed Aristotle), put knowledge into 'systems', written at great length as 'Summas'. The Franciscan way emphasised the will and contemplation as the basis of choice and moral action. The Dominican way emphasised the rational intellect. Thomas Aquinas developed the *Natural Law* theory which was to become a basis for all Roman Catholic moral theology.

Some features of Natural Law

- When it refers merely to the observed laws of nature, natural law is the basis of science.
- For moralists, Natural Law refers to the sense of *right* and *wrong* that comes from the use of reason. Goodness can be discovered by everyone as we are all given an intuitive mental capacity. Natural Law applies to everyone. It is only man-made laws that can apply to some people and not others.

- Natural Law rests on the idea that when God created the world he established an order within it. This was designed so that everything would move towards fulfilment.

- The natural purpose and function of something is the way God shows his will for it. This decides the basis for making moral choices. If it can be shown that something has a natural purpose, then to use it in an unnatural way is morally wrong (e.g. sexual intercourse can result, naturally, in pregnancy. To use contraceptives is seen as making sexual intercourse an unnatural action).

- In Natural Law it is the action itself that is defined morally, not its consequences. The end never justifies the means. The act can be justified even if its results are disastrous (as in the Pope's ban on the use of condoms in countries torn by the Aids epidemic). It is a deontological moral system, not a teleological one.

This moral system was challenged later, especially by William of Ockam (d. 1359) who favoured an ethical legalism, with God inventing moral rules. Moral duty was reduced to fulfilment of these obligations.

The sixteenth century

Martin Luther (d. 1546) challenged this legalism, and saw perfection less as an obligation and more as an ideal to be lived through God's grace. The Catholic Church's response to the various Protestant movements of this century was made at the *Council of Trent* (1545-1563).

The aim of Trent was to defend Catholic doctrine against the Reformers. Moral theology was placed alongside Canon Law and liturgical rubrics. Clear rules of behaviour were demanded with penalties for failure (e.g. for not saying the Divine Office). The sinfulness of actions was put into categories. *Sin* was highlighted and manuals written to help priests train as good 'confessors'. Their task was to form the consciences of penitents. Such a system was bound to result in a negative moral climate: 'How far can I go to live within the law?' There was an assumed certainty about right and wrong behaviour, with no exploration into the complexity of individual human life and moral theology was isolated from spirituality and Scripture. It was only concerned with law – revealed, natural, canon and civil. Scripture was used only to prove the Natural Law theory.

The Second Vatican Council (1963-65)

This reploughed the whole field of moral theology and its legalistic tradition. The Council Fathers did not produce a document on moral theology, but the whole tone of the Council indicated a shift away from legalism. Some of the most significant shifts in theology are found in the short document on Divine Revelation (*Dei Verbum*). Revelation was seen as broader than a set of propositions. The bishops accepted the ideas of theologians, like Karl Rahner and Bernard Lonergan, that God reveals *himself*, rather than ideas about himself; and that this revelation is discovered less in the mind than in the whole human experience of life.

Gaudium et Spes

These ideas were developed in the longest document of the Council, the 'Pastoral Constitution on the Church in the World Today' (*Gaudium et Spes*). The document was not planned in advance, but was drawn up as the Council progressed and it became evident that the real world in which we live needed a new appraisal. The document offers a dramatic move away from legalistic morality. The world is no longer described as a place of temptation and sin, but as a 'stage in human history . . . kept in being by its Creator's love'.

The Council's thinking about moral behaviour shifted away from rules and boundaries, to a process of conversion, centred on love. The world was no longer seen as a finished, unchangeable product, but as changeable, developing and diverse. The document speaks of 'reading the signs of the times'. This shift away from certainties suggests that moral norms should be applied tentatively with a new openness to revision, since today's complex world reveals new questions, and new problems.

After the Council

Gaudium et Spes was the Council's most hopeful outcome for many Catholics. It looks outward at humanity and focuses on modern living and the social issues that dominate society: medical ethics, war, development of culture, socio-economics, world poverty, politics and family life. This was a break away from the past. The analysis of modern attitudes must use insights drawn from sociology and psychology. Moreover, this document was set within the context of Scripture rather than the philosophy of Natural Law which for so long had been the only basis for social morality.

For several decades since, theologians and the laity have been asking new questions, and reconsidering the old answers. *The Catechism of the Catholic Church* (1994) adopted the new insight by rooting the moral life in discipleship of Christ. The truly 'moral' decision is to choose 'life' in its fullness, which is to be found in the Kingdom of God. Part III of the Catechism is in two sections.

- The first section looks at the dignity of the human person and the importance of the human community. Love of God cannot be separated from love of neighbour. Sin, personal and social, is described, and the importance of a right conscience is emphasised. The Natural Law theory is still described as the norm for leading us into responsible freedom. God's revealed laws are expressed in the Ten Commandments and the fulfilment of the New Law in Christ. The section ends with the reminder that our moral life is missionary by nature, building up the Church and the Kingdom.

- The second section focuses on the exhortation that we love God and our neighbour, by examining the Ten Commandments. It allows for more detailed examination of actual moral issues like abortion, homosexual acts, institutional injustices, drug abuse, fraud, etc.

The Catechism does not totally change the Church's traditional shape of moral theology. But what it does, in the spirit of Vatican II, is to place it firmly within the spirit of the Gospels. Moral life is seen as a response to God's invitation, in Christ, to a fullness of life. It begins and ends in the love of God, and thus calls Christians to lives of compassion. We are on a journey and need sustaining through prayer and the Eucharist, which is seen as the source and summit of the moral life. Conscience confers on us a profound personal dignity on this journey.

What is conscience?

The Council document *Gaudium et Spes* describes conscience this way:

> Deep within his conscience man discovers a law which he has not laid upon himself but which he must obey. Its voice, ever calling him to love and to do what is good and to avoid evil, sounds in his heart at the right moment . . . For man has in his heart a law inscribed by God . . . His conscience is man's most secret core and sanctuary. There he is alone with God whose voice echoes in his depths. (*Gaudium et Spes* 16)

The word 'conscience' is used in secular and in religious moral arguments. St Paul, when writing to the Romans, described it as 'the voice of God'. Thomas Aquinas was to call conscience 'the mind of man passing moral judgement'. More recent theologians have added emotional elements, insisting that conscience is not merely intellectual: emotions and will can contribute to moral judgements. The Council Fathers suggest this in the quotation above, by speaking of the heart and of the voice 'calling him to love'. This does not mean reducing conscience to a subjective inner 'feeling', or to Freud's *superego*, which relies on guilt to bring about a judgement.

The formation of a right conscience depends on two things: freedom and the ability to distinguish right from wrong. Without freedom it is impossible to make a choice. The debate amongst moralists and psychologists is how far this sense of right and wrong is innate. Is it acquired only through teaching and example? The Church has always spoken of the need to 'form' a good conscience.

A well-formed conscience is upright and truthful. It formulates its judgements according to reason, in conformity with the true good willed by the wisdom of the Creator. Everyone must avail himself of the means to form his conscience. (*Catechism of the Catholic Church* 1798)

In short, Catholics have the responsibility to make a serious effort to incorporate the moral vision of the *Church* when they make ethical choices. As we have seen, the Church's moral vision is based on Scripture, tradition and the exercise of magisterium.

Christian morality and the Bible

Since Vatican II, Catholics have been encouraged to turn to the Scriptures for guidance. But there is a problem in turning to the Bible for answers on ethical questions. All too often sacred writings, of any world religion, can be used to justify wrong actions. These writings do not have one agreed answer to moral questions. Some Christians think that the Old Testament can still provide common principles laid down by the prophets, and others turn only to the New Testament to find authoritative guidance there. Some even presume that certain Old Testament rules are actually binding (e.g. on homosexuality).

This is rather naïve. To use certain texts to give *direct* answers to moral problems ignores the recent revolution in biblical studies. There will always be some absolutes – the Ten Commandments, for example, remain the moral checklist for all societies. But most scholars recognise that the Bible must be used with caution. A distressed woman, interviewed on television about the murder of her son, said that only the death penalty would do as punishment for the killer. 'The Bible says "an eye for an eye",' she said, 'so I want a life for a life.' You cannot appeal to the Bible in this way.

The Old and New Testaments are historically conditioned, and need to be interpreted in the light of the problems they were dealing with then. It is a mistake to say, 'the Bible says', or 'the Bible forbids'. Times change, and new discoveries require new interpretations.

Even the prescriptions laid down by the early Christians were adapted within the New Testament itself. For example:

- To the absolute ruling on divorce in Mark 10:9, Matthew adds an exception ten years or so later – Matthew 5:32, 19:9.
- Mark 10:17f demands total poverty from Jesus' followers. Paul and Luke simply urge followers to be generous. One hundred years later, Clement of Alexandria says Jesus told the rich man only to be detached from his wealth, not give it up.

So the historical study of the New Testament and early Church shows its ethics in a new light. We no longer have a series of commands to obey, but simply a record of the various ways in which the early Christians solved their ethical problems. We should not universalise. Sadly, few Catholics today have any knowledge of recent biblical scholarship. It is no wonder they are confused about contemporary moral issues. The Bible, after all, does not mention contraception or ecology. Some continue to quote the Bible as 'thou shalts' and 'thou shalt nots'. Others, confused, reject the New Testament as a moral guide saying it was only relevant for its time. Some say that its general principles are applicable for all time. But how do we decide what these general principles are?

The balance is best kept by holding both ends, not dropping one or the other. One end is the Christian origins in the Jesus of the New Testament, the other is the present world situation. Our Christian origins cannot dictate our behaviour to us, but we cannot call ourselves Christian if we do not pay attention to Jesus as both inspiration and corrective. We read the New Testament as believers. In Jesus we encounter the divine and this aspect cannot be ignored.

But the present situation in which we live is also God's gift, demanding a response here and now. The New Testament cannot make that response for us. We must make our own responsible decisions. In short, we cannot simply repeat the words and ideas of the Bible as if it were not thousands of years old. But neither can we simply ignore it as irrelevant. We have to ask: 'If they, in their circumstances, came to these conclusions, what conclusions must I come to in my circumstances?' By looking at an example of a practical moral issue we will discover that even this approach is not easy.

The sanctity of life

All Christians agree that life is sacred. Each person is unique and blessed – by being created in the 'image of God'. For this reason the Catholic Church has always taken an uncompromising position over moral issues that involve choosing *for* life. The Catholic Church takes an absolute position on the sanctity of life from which it then speaks on particular matters. The case of the Siamese twins in 2001 demonstrated this. (Mary's life was sacrificed to give life to her sister Jodie. Without medical intervention both would have died.) The Church opposed this decision.

Recently two women sought permission from the courts to choose their own time to die. One was so debilitated that she needed assistance from her husband, who was willing to help her die. Although she was in pain and losing dignity, she could survive longer with the help of drugs. The Law Lords denied permission for her husband to help her commit suicide. Archbishop Peter Smith of Cardiff is Chair of the Catholic Department of Christian Responsibility and Citizenship. In this capacity he made a public statement:

> No one can fail to be moved by the suffering of Diane Pretty and her husband . . . We are bound to alleviate sufferings but it is always wrong to intentionally kill innocent human beings. The Law Lords have rightly upheld the longstanding prohibition, against euthanasia and assisted suicide, which exists, among other things, to protect the weak and vulnerable members of society.

The couple then took the case to the European Court of Human Rights, which also opposed the request. Diane died soon after.

The second woman was in a similar state, but could not survive without the artificial help of a ventilator. The British courts agreed to her request. The Pope told a meeting of leading doctors why he agreed with this:

Continued medical treatment, even with the best intentions, would not only be futile but also not respectful to the patient who had reached a terminal stage. Carry on with your research into new techniques and medicine but do not forget that Man is a limited and mortal being. Educating people to accepting their death serenely is ▸also part of your mission. Not only must the body be taken into account, but also the spirit. (Lecture notes, Pope John Paul II)

The press seems surprised at Pope John Paul's words. But the view has always been held by the Church (see *Catechism of the Catholic Church* 2278) and was expressed clearly by the Pope in his encyclical *Evangelium Vitae*, that the patient has the right to forgo 'aggressive medical treatment that would only secure a precarious and burdensome prolongation of life, so long as the normal care due to the sick person in similar cases is not interrupted' (65).

This does not contradict the Church's clear opposition to 'direct euthanasia' which is 'an act or omission which, of itself or by intention, causes death in order to eliminate suffering' (*Catechism of the Catholic Church*).

Some Catholics have wondered why it has taken so long for the Church to have doubts about the morality of accepting the death penalty. With the Gospel insistence on forgiveness and generosity towards the sinner, it seems strange that the Church accepted that some lives *could* be cut short on the result of human judgements about behaviour. Are sinners' lives less precious than those of the terminally sick or the unborn? The original text on capital punishment in the *Catechism of the Catholic Church* caused some concern for many Catholics. As a result, the issue was reassessed and changes were made. In a recent edition of the Catechism this is mentioned on the dust cover: 'The original text on capital punishment provoked a wide-ranging debate which led to further clarification in the encyclical *Evangelium Vitae*. Thus the original sentence on capital punishment has been omitted, reflecting a developing consensus within the Catholic Christian community against this practice.' This is most interesting evidence that the views of the whole Church are being considered and taken into account by the Vatican.

It is on the issue of *abortion* that the Catholic Church is unwavering.

From as early as the second century the message has been the same: 'You shall not kill a child by abortion, nor kill at birth' (*The Didache*). The majority of Catholics today believe that it is morally wrong to terminate directly life in the womb. It was not until the second half of the twentieth century that the Catholic position on abortion was challenged. The secular and medical world began to accept abortion in some circumstances. The Abortion Law was passed in England in 1967. In response, the Church reaffirmed its teaching with vigour. In 1974 the *Congregation for the Doctrine of the Faith* issued a 'Declaration on Procured Abortion', which was backed up by the 1983 revision of Canon Law that states: 'A person who procures a completed abortion incurs an automatic excommunication' (Canon 1398).

In 1991 a meeting of 'experts on human life' was called in Rome by the Pontifical Council for the Family. The 'experts' reaffirmed an earlier statement in the 1974 Instruction, *Donum Vitae*, that the unborn 'must be respected and treated as a human person'. The same document stated that: 'From the time the ovum is fertilised, a new life is begun which is neither that of the father nor the mother; it is rather the life of a new human being with its own growth.'

Document after Church document repeats this view in uncompromising language. But some Catholic moralists and laity are asking questions. Theologians, like Charles Curran, Richard McCormick, Bernard Häring and Karl Rahner, have been open to research made in reproductive biology. The scientists believe that it is unlikely that an individual human life can be present until two or three weeks after fertilisation. (It takes 21 days before two important stages in the development of the embryo are complete.) The question, 'When does human life begin?' is a crucial one. Those who accept the biologists' hesitations will have some grounds to allow for the *Situation Ethic* view that, in extreme circumstances, like rape or incest, it would be permissible to remove the early embryo or take the *morning-after* pill. The majority, however, argue that as human life is so sacred it must be protected at all stages, including 'potential human life'. The Church does accept that a therapeutic abortion can be allowed. This is when abortion is a necessity to save the life of the mother, in an ectopic pregnancy, for example, or if she has cancer of the uterus. This would constitute an indirect abortion.

Some Catholics, whilst sharing the Church's view on abortion, are uneasy about the central role this one issue seems to hold in the mind of some groups and the Catholic media. It suggests that emotions can play a large part in making this moral choice. The language and visuals used in advertisements and propaganda material are sometimes inappropriate and have led some schools to hesitate to invite speakers from *Life* or *SPUC* (Society for the Protection of the Unborn Child). There are those who find it puzzling that some pro-life supporters seem to have little to say about the violation of human rights in many world situations that condemn innocent lives – especially of the young – to tragic and early deaths. These Catholics say that the *right to life* issue should surely be taken seriously in its broadest sense.

Some Catholics are caught between the Church's teaching and their conscience in this regard. Catholic field-workers in Africa, for example, are taking a lead in the fight against Aids. They see no other way than the utilitarian practice of supplying condoms to prevent the crisis becoming an 'epidemic'. The Pope does not approve.

There is positive evidence, from recent papal statements and from the writings of contemporary theologians, that the Church is widening its vision and listening to the secular world with greater sensitivity than in the past. The Catholic Church has an important role to play in participating in moral debate with a world that is struggling with life issues – war, economics, ecology, family life, violence, inequality, the plight of refugees and immigrants, poverty and lack of human rights.

Some ideas for discussion groups or essay titles

- How should conscience and moral norms be interrelated? Why does *Veritatis Splendor* insist that some acts are morally disordered?

- In what way is the Natural Law teaching of Vatican II (*Gaudium et Spes*, Part 1) developed by Pope John Paul II in his encyclicals *Veritatis Splendor* and *Evangelium Vitae*?
- How far are the insights and teachings of Vatican II (*Gaudium et Spes*, Part 2, Chapter 1) reflected and developed in the *Catechism of the Catholic Church*?
- 'The only way to deal with the population explosion is by compulsory birth control.' The Catholic Church would not agree. Why is this, and what solution does the Church offer?
- Research the most recent questions raised in medical ethics (e.g. cloning), and explain the position taken by the Catholic Church.

Further reading

Catechism of the Catholic Church, Chapman, 1994.

Hayes, M. and Gearon, L. *Contemporary Catholic Theology: A Reader*, (pages 369-433), Gracewing, 2001.

Hughes, G., SJ, *Moral Decisions*, Gill and Macmillan, 1989.

MacNamara, V. *The Truth in Love: Reflections on Christian Morality*, Gill and Macmillan, 1989.

Macquarrie, J. and Childress, J. (eds), *A New Dictionary of Christian Ethics*, SCM Press, 1986.

Pinckaers, S., OP, *Morality: The Catholic View*, St Augustine's Press, 2001.

Pope John Paul II, *Veritatis Splendor*, CTS.

See also: *Pastoral Constitution: Gaudium et Spes, Vatican II* and various encyclicals mentioned in the text.

Notes for those writing essays

It may be a few years since some of you wrote essays for a tutor. Here are a few reminders or tips that you may find helpful.

- Read the question several times until you are quite sure what is being asked.

- Be aware that in your answer you will need to show you have both a good *knowledge* of the subject and a clear *understanding* of the issues, and are able to *evaluate and apply* the information to the contemporary world and your own situation.

- *Knowledge*: Read as much as you can about the subject, and make rough notes. Get hold of some of the recommended books.

- *Understanding*: Test your understanding by reading a section of a book or an article, then close the book and write a short summary of what you read. Discuss the topic with family or friends. Meet with others who are doing the course and have your own discussion.

- *Evaluation and application*: Make sure you look at the topic from all sides. Write down the pros and cons of attitudes taken, or of views expressed by theologians or moralists, etc. Collect articles from the media on relevant issues.

- Make a plan of your essay. Sort out the material you have collected and see where to put it. Write an interesting introduction (you can use a quotation, or an incident that is related to the main argument of your question). Send this plan to your tutor for approval before you go any further.

- Write your essay in full. Always keep your eye on the wording of the question, and don't stray off the point. Write in simple, and uncomplicated sentences.

- Never just copy out bits and pieces from what you have read. Make it your own, and show you understand and can apply it to your situation (in the classroom, the parish, the catechetical group, etc.).

- Make the essay 'human', by including stories, quotations, or real situations (as long as they are relevant).

- Acknowledge all your sources, and add a bibliography. This should include articles taken from the Internet.

Acknowledgements

The publishers wish to thank all those who have given their permission to reproduce copyright material in this publication.

Page 36: Quote from *Documents of Vatican II*, ed. Walter Abbott. © Herder & Herder 1966.

Page 36, 43: John O'Grady, *Contemporary Catholic Theology*, ed. Michael Hayes & Liam Geardon, 1998. © Gracewing, 2 Southern Ave, Leominster, Herefordshire HR6 0QF. Used by permission.

Page 45: Quote from *Enchiridion Symbolorum*, Henry Denziger, translated by H. J. Richards. Herder & Co, 1937. © Marian House, Powers Lake, North Dakota, USA.

Page 50: Raymond Brown, *The Churches the Apostles Left Behind*. © 1984, Paulist Press. Used with permission of Paulist Press.

Page 54: Hans Küng, *The Church*, Search Press, 1967. © Search Press. Used by permission of Continuum International Publishing Group Ltd, The Tower Building, 11 York Road, London SE1 7NX.

Pages 59, 82, 97: *The Catechism of the Catholic Church*. English translation. © Geoffrey Chapman, an imprint of Cassell plc. Original Latin text © Liberia Editrice Vaticana. Used by permission of Cassell plc, Wellington House, 125 Strand, London WC2R 0BB.

Page 61: Adrian Smith, *Tomorrow's Parish*, 1983. © Adrian Smith. Used by permission.

Page 61: Sister Pamela Hussey, HCJ, *A New Way of Being Church*. © The Grail, 1986. Used by permission of The Grail (England).

Page 63: Bishop Butler, *The Theology of Vatican II*. Published and © 1981, by Darton, Longman & Todd, 1 Spencer Court, 140-142 Wandsworth High Street, London SW18 4JJ. Used by permission.

Page 64: Quote from *The Catholic Gazette*, the monthly journal of the Catholic Missionary Society (November 1956). Used by permission.

Page 70: Fr Hugh Lavery, *Sacraments*. Published and © 1982, by Darton, Longman & Todd, 1 Spencer Court, 140-142 Wandsworth High Street, London SW18 4JJ.

Page 71: Chased-by-Bears (Yanktonai Sioux), *Native American Wisdom.* © Running Press, Philadelphia, USA, 1994.

Pages 73, 77: Quotes from *Course notes for CCRS*, Diocese of East Anglia. © Maurice Lynch. Used by permission.

Page 84: Damian Lundy, from *To Live Is To Change*, Jamison, Lundy and Poole, Rejoice Publications, 1995. © Rejoice Publications, 19 Wellington Close, Chelmsford, Essex CM1 2EE. Used by permission.

Page 91: Fr Kevin Dring, from a lecture to permanent deacons in training, Wonersh, 2002. Used by kind permission of Fr Kevin Dring.

Page 100: Lecture notes, Pope John Paul II. © L'Osservatore Romano, Rome.

All quotations from translations of Vatican documents used by kind permission of the Catholic Truth Society, 40-46 Harleyford Road, London SE11 5AY.